Barn Bo

Brian J. Ward

The recommendations, advice, descriptions and the methods described in this book are presented solely for educational purposes. The author and publisher assume no liability whatsoever for any loss or damage that results from the use of any of the material in this book. Use of the material in this book is solely at the risk of the user.

Author/Managing Editor: Brian J. Ward

Reviewers:

Staff Sergeant Wayne Husband II - U.S. Air Force, Retired
Fire Chief Devon Wells, Hood River Fire Department (OR)
Battalion Chief David Rhodes, City of Atlanta Fire Rescue (GA)

ISBN 9780692638941 (paperback), First Edition

Published August 2016

Printed in North Charleston, South Carolina
United States of America

If your actions inspire others to dream more, learn more, do more and become more, you are a leader.

John Quincy Adams

Preface

What is Leadership? What does it mean to lead? Leadership is about breaking "stuff." This "stuff" could be rules, behaviors, cultures, change, and a host of other topics. The Barn Boss has to determine what is worth breaking and are we doing it for the right reasons. In overly simplistic terms, leadership is the means of leading an individual or a group towards a common goal, having a vision, if you will. Having the ability to influence people when there's nothing holding them to listen to what you have to say, furthermore it's the ability to get the job done effectively and efficiently with the least amount of energy possible. Retired Phoenix Fire Chief Alan Brunacini provides the following information on the Barn Boss (Alan calls this the functional boss) concept concerning the leadership ability in reference to the team – *"The ability of the boss to manage organizational resources in a way that improves the performance and the positive behavior of the individuals and their teams directly increases the personal respect they receive. When this occurs, that person brings that legitimate performance based respect to this team and that increases everyone's collective capability = synergy. This is what bringing out the best really means."*

Some believe that leaders are born such as by nature to be great while others, such as myself, believe that leaders are groomed to succeed. In the November 2015 edition of Fire Engineering, Editor-in-Chief Bobby Halton, as he so often does, eloquently described a great firefighter as possessing the "particular blend of authority and morality that connotes competence, good manners, restraint, and elitism." Some of this is derived from our parents and the environment we are born into. While the other aspects are delivered through mentoring, training, and examples.

This book is a compilation of application, science, tradition, history, fire and psychology blended to fit inside the firehouse for every firefighter. The content of this book crosses all generations, ranks and years of seniority. If you are motivated and inspired to learn like the best, train like the best, and be the best – this book is for you. The fire service is one of, if not the most, storied histories of all industries in the world. Organizations around the world strive to replicate our public image and develop leaders such as those of the fire service.

When I first let my intentions be known that I wanted to try being an recruit school instructor the first comment that I heard from the guys was, "Hey, Brian, don't you have to talk to teach!" Wise words from the funny guy at Station 24, Matt Cook. The ability to be able to influence someone is nothing more than having a well thought out, planned purpose and being able to effectively communicate that purpose or vision. We will motivate others to become involved in assisting the Fire Service overcome our obstacles and become more involved in helping us prevent needless injuries and deaths. We also want it to be known that even the 2, 3, and 4 year seasoned firefighter can have a huge impact not just on their department but on the service as a whole.

Before we go too far though, how do we get to that point of influencing people, especially, as the low man on the totem pole (from a formal rank)? Mentoring is a big part of it; I had extremely great mentors that pushed me from day one to right now. They showed me and taught me that it was ok to make a difference. It is much easier to accept this new guy when people know where your heart is. These mentors were willing to listen, they were also willing to let me go out there and maybe fail, but they helped me learn why some things worked and other things did not work. Some I figured out on my own, but for a lot of it I had to be explained how to obtain what I wanted to accomplish and was encouraged to go after it.

Throughout this book we will look at several items that will tell what the Barn Boss is and its impact on you as an individual and as a team member. Colleague and friend Dawson County (GA) Fire Chief Lanier Swafford said "Develop your priorities based upon what can make the greatest impact upon your department, our profession and most importantly – individuals." There are many different aspects of leadership that apply at all levels, no matter what age or rank an individual may be. The stories and experiences that I have faced, which you may be facing right now or in the future, will help you navigate your own potential outcomes. Hopefully, some of the stories and analogies will help you make a decision in where you want to take your career or start your career in my case.

So, I decided to write about Leadership from the Little Guy or what I am now calling Barn Boss Leadership, the individual that doesn't have 30 years on the job and the individual which doesn't carry a chief officer rank. I chose to write the first article because of what I felt I was able to accomplish may help other firefighters. Now I am focusing my efforts on compiling all of the experiences up to this point in my life for others to learn. This is about sharing information and knowledge, it's about making sure everyone goes home, and letting the new generation of firefighters know that they can make a difference, they can lead.

I'm not saying that my path was right or it was the best way to go but it has worked for me. Hopefully, I can pass along something that will encourage everyone to be a little more motivated than before and to take care of each other, remember this is a family and you have to believe it with your heart. Brotherhood! There is no other profession like it.

Acknowledgments

I want to thank several individuals that are directly related to any success I may have seen. I owe everything to them. You will get to meet some of these characters throughout the book. Mark Peters - Always had words of wisdom. Wayne Mooney - Thanks for keeping me in the loop. Chuck "Chucky" Barnwell - the conversations that we have had... Casey Synder - one of my first mentors, thanks for taking the time to teach me. Ron Dennis and Billy Hayes - thanks for your support throughout the years. David Rhodes – "Smoke Daddy" thanks for the time you gave up to help some kid and for the challenge. John Norman - thanks for sharing your knowledge, passion and the ride around NY. Eddie Buchannan – thank you for the opportunities and guidance. Mull, Pollock, Shepperd, Wolfe, Rowan - some of the best company officers I've ever worked for and to all of the individuals that have guided me and opened doors for me, thank you. I didn't forget you, Jug, my first Barn Boss and Doug Stephenson – the PT Asshole.

This is for my family which has always been there for me – Dad, Mom, Jerry, Scott, Wesley and Brooke - Thank You. This book is also in memory of Uncle Danny and TJ. One hell of an Uncle and Retired Army Green Beret Staff Sergeant. And to TJ, childhood and family friends, who perished serving his community – EOW 5/6/2016.

Be Safe, Train Hard and Take Care
Brian Ward

Barn Boss Leadership

"Make the Difference"

Chapter 1

"When you think that you have done everything, there is always one more thing you can do."

Lieutenant General Hal Moore

What the hell is a Barn Boss?

What and who is the Barn Boss? Some of you may be asking what the hell a barn has to do with anything in the fire service. There were numerous reasons for choosing the Barn Boss terminology, specifically due to its relevance to the fire service and the tradition that comes with it. Tradition is lost in the minds of many firefighters and from the firehouses themselves. I understand that some traditions need to go but some need to stay, we need to remember where we came from; the struggles, the good times and the bad times within each fire department and in the fire service as a whole. These are the avenues that we as firefighters learn from and they make us stronger as an individual. If we ever lose sight of where we come from, we lose touch with reality. We become oblivious to the situations surrounding us, and allow our fire departments to fall to ruins and our firefighter's morale to lose the strong foundation needed for this job. For these very reasons, I decided pay homage to our traditions and use a part of our storied history for the title, the term Barn Boss was born.

Think back to what it must have been like to be the individual responsible for taking care of the horses, making sure their every need was satisfied and they were ready to leave at a moment's notice. The tools were all in their proper place, sanded, painted and sharpened. The bridles and reins are neatly prepared and the leather is oiled. The wheels, spokes and integrity of the wagon has been inspected. The horses have been fed, properly trained, and rested.

It is much like how we operate today; we simply traded fine thoroughbred horses for custom cab pumpers and truck companies. We still have the seasoned firefighters and driver/engineers that perform the same vital functions in today's technologically advanced fire stations with turbo boast engines and electronic transmissions. This is where the Barn Boss comes in, this is your go-to guy or gal, the individual that makes sure everyone is trained up, squared away, and ready to run. Trumpets do not have to exist for a Barn Boss and neither does 30 years of seniority. These are the individuals that are running the station behind the scene. These are the same individuals that can use their influence to affect positive changes in crews, stations, departments and geographical regions. They lead the crews without being told and they are your up-and-comers.

My first Barn Boss, David Jugenhiemer or "Jug" for short because we could barely pronounce it – much less spell it, (you have to feel for this guy's kids growing with a last name like that) he was the driver at our technical rescue station, Station 24, and I was a two or three-year firefighter at that point in my career. We didn't call him the "Barn Boss" but he made sure everything happened and taught others to make sure everything happened. The odd part, with his over grown Fu Manchu, is that if you could get him to be serious for 10 minutes you really accomplished something. There was always a joke to be told or some fun to be had. When he was making stuff happen it was never accomplished through intimidation or fear. It was his knowledge and personality that made him who he was. He also was a pretty damn good cook, which never hurts in the fire station. I still cook Italian sagetti' to this day the way I learned from Jug.

Look around the fire service and you will see these individuals everywhere, they are the movers and shakers of the fire service. They are in every department, even if we don't see it at first. Barn Bosses are expected to help firefighters find their way and to show them how to toe the line. Take them to the limits, show them what is possible with a little heart, teach them what a book and PowerPoint has no clue about. However, teach them to not be ignorant of science and research – to embrace it and explain to them the things that only a firefighter would ever understand. For example, what is a brotherhood? Show them brotherhood and all of the little intricacies that are beyond the concept of the public and, more than I would like to admit, some firefighters. This position has a proud and distinguished history placed on it, and I feel that it was important to keep in touch with that.

I want to take a second and give you a little background on where the information and the concept for Barn Boss came from as it has evolved over the last couple of years for me personally. Some may remember the launching of the first phase of this material at Fire Department Instructors Conference in 2011 and the original article published by Fire Engineering in September 2008 as Leadership from the Little Guy (Appendix 1). This article is important for more reasons than we have paper to write on, as it was the beginning of everything outside the bay walls. The bottom line for me personally was that Leadership from the Little Guy was the start of my exposure outside of Georgia and became one of the major benchmarks for my career. Taking this class on the road allowed me to start validating the principals and concepts that I lead my career by. It also opened myself up for challenge from others and allowed me to grow as a person. This is where the original concept and a fair amount of the material for the Barn Boss was developed.

If there was ever a place where business seems to get taken care of and ideas developed, it is the Fire Department Instructors Conference (FDIC). The knowledge that enters the convention center during that week is beyond belief. Even after several years of attending this conference and the chance to teach multiple times, I still do not know how to wrap my hands around all of it. There is more to do than you ever have time to accomplish and you spend the whole year trying to accomplish what happens in one week at FDIC. Holding true to this theory of mine, the Barn Boss was born over an adult beverage in a bar in downtown Indianapolis on the last teaching day of the conference with Hanover (VA) Division Chief Eddie Buchanan. The only way this story could get better was if I wrote the chapters out on a bar napkin (which is another story that happened in Emmitsburg (MD) with Horry County (SC) Assistant Chief Doug Cline). Doug and I were both board members for the International Society of Fire Service Instructors (ISFSI) and we wrote a five year plan on the dinner napkins of an Italian pub outside of Emmitsburg and then we would text them to Leigh Hubbard, ISFSI Executive Director, and wait for a response......

A great friend, mentor, colleague, drummer and just a good person, Eddie Buchanan asked the question, "What's the next challenge?" My initial reply was to simply be invited back to FDIC to teach again. I asked myself what else is there? For me, I will never have back my first presentation at FDIC, the nerves, the heart pulsating through my throat; it does not get any better than that. It was one of the most distinguished opportunities of my career, and an invite back – who knows. Fortunately, for me I have been honored to be invited back several times in various capacities from Hands on Training (HOT), workshops, logistics assistant and as a lead classroom instructor.

As our conversation developed through the night, the idea of the Barn Boss was developed from the presentation that I did earlier that day and then the mention of a book came about. From presentation to book was a huge jump but why not (keep in mind this is 2011). It took nearly 6 years to complete this book, some from a lack of ability to put thoughts and actions into words and then trying to live life – published a textbook, job change, master's degree, marriage, etc...

From the concept of being a Barn Boss or the original "Little Guy" materials – I'm talking about the individual that may not have rank or trumpets or veteran status. The Barn Boss possesses a direct influence, respect and a desire to lead by example. These characteristics and traits have nothing to do with position power or status and in most cases are much harder to obtain than when you're given the position power from a promotion. There comes a point as a Barn Boss where you have to prove yourself much more than the average firefighter or officer would ever have to do. There will come a time where all leaders, formal and informal, will be tested. The difference between successful outcomes and failures comes down to a few questions.

- First, how prepared are you to be a leader? Have you put forth the time and effort to learn the materials that you need to?
- Second, do you accept the responsibility for your decisions and can you justify them when challenged?
- Third, are you willing to perform everything that you ask of your crew to perform?

All situations have different variables that arise and plans have to be modified accordingly. However, if an individual can answer all of these questions with adequate substance as an informal leader, they have the chance to be successful. However, remember nothing worth having comes easy; a leader has to be prepared to go above and beyond. They set the tone and the bar for where everyone else must strive too.

The Informal Leader – a.k.a. Barn Boss

There are certain items that I have learned throughout my career that seem to hold true when discussing an informal leader's position. Topics such as Knowing and Doing Your Job, Pride, and Behavior Modeling, are all items that I could not justify writing this book if we did not discuss. As you contemplate the informal leader's role and even the transition to a formal leadership role I think we should all review the two statements below from two of the oldest leadership organizations in the world. Neither of them represent the command and control mentality, in fact, the Army Manual says "anyone" can be a leader if they possess the ability to inspire and influence. The Air Force Doctrine Document even goes as far to say that leadership does not equal command. This is a gut check for anyone in a leadership capacity or aspiring to a leadership role. The trumpets and stripes do not make the leader.

United States Army Manual defines the leader as "anyone who by virtue of assumed role or assigned responsibility inspires and influences people to accomplish organizational goals."

The Air Force Doctrine Document 1-1, Leadership and Force Development describes leadership as "Leadership is the art and science of influencing and directing people to accomplish the assigned mission." The document goes on to say that "Leadership does not equal command, but all commanders should be leaders."

"Know your Job, Do your Job"

So, how do you apply the Barn Boss concept and why choose this mentality? I am using this quote from Gwinnett County Fire and Emergency Services Retired Fire Chief Bill Myers, one of the items that is preached during promotion sit downs in this department is, "Know your job, Do your job." This saying embodies what and who the Barn Boss stands for. They are the individual that is the go-to-person; they know their job and practice carrying it out every day. This is done even though they perform every action to a flawless point; they expect precision with every move. This is exactly where this concept comes from, simple enough, but for various reasons it seems to be difficult at times to follow this saying, for some. We all have other priorities in life that we have to handle and mitigate, but there is no excuse for the individuals that sit at the fire station all day and the only muscle that is worked out is from working the remote. We have to be more than that, because we are more than that!

Practice Doesn't Make Perfect

When you train individually or as a team – is it a check the box type of day or is it a this could really happen type of day? It's very easy to check the box in our daily lives and make everything a routine. Wake up, shower, coffee, drive to work, check the box for minimum expectations, go home, etc.... If you fall into this mentality it can be personally and professionally devastating at the extremes. However, even if nothing "bad" ever happens I challenge you to contemplate how much you are missing from the big picture. How much knowledge and skills could you be passing on to the next generation if you took the time to go beyond the check box? Practice will never make me, you or anyone else perfect – Perfect Practice beyond the Mastery Level will make us Perfect.

During the 2015 Fire Department Instructors Conference (FDIC), Retired Rear Admiral Scott Moore presented "Building No Fail Teams," for no fail missions. Admiral Moore had served in every Seal Team capacity from the ground up from 1984 until his retirement in 2014. He described the lead up to the SEAL Team 6 raid that rescued an America hostage in Somalia in 2012 (this happens to be the same team that exterminated Bin Laden). Before this mission started, you have to go back to 2010. He described that in order for the Navy Seals to be a no fail team they had to train to be such. Typically, they spend 18 months training for a six month deployment. 18 months practicing the same skills over and over, in different capacities for what may or may not happen. The skills and knowledge was put to the test through constant stress. They stressed their muscles and their minds. They were forced to make decisive decisions, without fail. The mentality has to be more than just checking the box – their lives and the lives of their comrades depend on it.

For those in the fire service, I encourage you to research the Georgia Smoke Divers (GSD) Association. Their training is designed around this concept just as Seal Team 6 is. It is tough and grueling training as they stress your muscles and mind, and then give you a scenario that will always require you to adapt and overcome. The knowledge and skills obtained through this class are basic skills executed beyond perfection. GSD – "Strong in Mind and Body."

This process requires instituting the Overlearning Theory into application. Regardless if you're on Seal Team 6, a professional athlete or a firefighter the theory applies. The one item in common between all three is that their skill level cannot be flawed. The Overlearning Theory is defined as practice beyond mastery. When we learn

"Practice Beyond Mastery"

past mastery, we are able to adapt our knowledge and skills more readily when the situation changes unexpectedly. As well, overlearning ensures that the skills are more automatic (samurai like instincts). Go back to Seal Team 6 in Somalia; upon arrival to the pirate camp ground they encountered gun fire. While they trained for it and surely prepared, did they know exactly where and how the attack would come? They were able to adapt to the situation based on their overlearning. When you respond to a house fire, surely you trained for it, but, can you adapt to the situation without making a mistake? Seal Team 6 walked away with two hostages, no causalities and nine dead pirates.

Werner and Dismone describe in detail the Building No Fail Teams concept by providing the following example: "Soldiers repeatedly practice their maneuvers and task, so when orders come to attack, these tasks will be second nature and can be performed quickly and correctly." Furthermore, Daniel Willingham states that "Practice makes perfect, only if you practice beyond the point of perfection." Does this sound like something ALL should consider in the fire service? Many of you already practice and apply this concept, even without calling it No Fail or Overlearning. However, for those that believe that raising a ladder once a year will prepare you for raising a ladder when the stress of a rescue is standing in front of you, you are greatly mistaken. Train as if your life depends on it in everything you do. Be Seal Team 6 in your organization.

Obviously, knowing your job encompasses a lot of reading, training, and staying current on new trends in the service. We can do that, it is fairly simple with all of the core competencies, and quarterly training required, hell, we can sit around the kitchen table talking in the morning and train! Useful training, at that! Ol' Reliable, throw a fire service magazine, especially a Fire Engineering magazine, on the table. Study it for a second and break down the picture with all of its possibilities or use the Lessons Learned Case Studies. Put yourself in their place. Fire Chief Scott Thompson (2014), discusses making it personal in his Training

Basics article, which it is his experience that training which impacts the emotional/personal level produces the best results.

Below is an excerpt from my FDIC 2016 Workshop Developing Tactical Decision Games (TDG) where we use the kitchen table and a magazine for training.

Tactical Decision Games – Fire Engineering Magazine Hot Seat:

Take a magazine with any incident and study what it is telling you. For example, a particular picture may provide training on building construction, fire behavior, flow paths, tactics, and reading smoke to name a few. Sitting at the kitchen table, tell everyone what you are about to do, so they are prepared. Next, pick a student and unveil the cover of the magazine. Allow 2 – 10 seconds (depending on knowledge level – never try to embarrass anyone) for review and then start the rapid fire of questions. As they answer one, provide the next without hesitation. Your questions should be determined prior to the training session. It generally works well to have four or five magazines available so that each crewmember is actively involved with a different situation. This method is really no cost to the students (small subscription cost – ask your department to purchase, as most will) and is very quick to development. Sample questions to consider:

- Provide a size-up based on Side A information.
- What is your first consideration?
- Where is the fire traveling?
- What color is the smoke / what is it telling you?
- Is Vent-Enter-Isolate-Search an option?

Adaptability

It's also important to remember that the incident commander (IC) or leader may be faced with changing situations and environments, conflicting reports and information or simply new information that will change the outcome of the incident. In this case be flexible, allow the leader to do their job and be open to switching assignments if needed or backing out of the structure all together. You may not always get to be on the nozzle or be the one pulling ceiling but it may be because you're too valuable with your searches, being a safety officer or division leader yourself. Whatever the case, be prepared to act and adapt accordingly.

There were two manpower squads in my pervious department, each carries specialized equipment with four personnel and there is always a paramedic assigned to the squad. One of the squads is assigned to every structure fire, no matter where in the county it may be. Most of the time, not always, they are assigned as the Rapid Intervention Crew (RIC). This is simply because they have the most manpower and the equipment readily available to handle such a situation. However, on occasions they are assigned as fire attack, search, ventilation and every other fire ground job. They have to be flexible, probably more so than most because they expect to be RIC and once they pull up they may be assigned to some other task. This capability and adaptability allows a tremendous amount of leeway to our leaders and IC's with what they can do and accomplish on-scene. We should be this way in every situation, on and off the incident scene.

There is also another aspect of knowing your job that most don't think about. There is the challenge of learning what each of your crew members bring to the table. When we do this, we also have to think about life experience, not just what they have experienced in the field. Explore each of them and find out what they know. What is their knowledge level? What are their strengths and weaknesses? They may possess the one piece of information or knowledge that you don't have. Point in case; I go back to about 2010:

I was riding as the Acting Officer with a first month rookie and a two-year relief driver. We were dispatched to an industrial accident where a man had climbed over the trip wire (Mistake – Never climb over a trip wire) to make an adjustment near two steel rollers. Unfortunately, he never did get to make the adjustment before he found two steel rollers arm deep. When we arrived on scene the maintenance crews were already there but were unable to free the worker. The call was made for additional manpower and to deliver some specialized equipment on scene. The first weapon that I had was a 45-year-old rookie that was a licensed electrician – who better to do a de-energization validation. The second weapon and the one that freed the individual was a then Captain (now Battalion Chief Chuck Amason) that had experience as a mechanic in his backyard and knew how to use a three prong pull system. A 3 prong pull is a mechanical device used to pull gears apart. Our fire service experience left much to be desired on this call, however, knowing the life experiences of the firefighters around us can greatly benefit every call that we run. This eventually made the Fire Engineering article Always be Prepared for the Unexpected in 2012. A similar incident occurred in 2011 with a similar crew set up where we were first on scene of a Hydrogen Sulfide suicide, at the time it was the third publicly documented incident in the country. I later wrote the Lessons Learned from Hydrogen Sulfide Incident in 2011 for Fire Engineering.

As the Barn Boss, it is your job to make sure that you know these qualities and the only way to find out the qualities of your crew is to get outside and train. Ask questions, find out their strengths and weaknesses, and don't be afraid to offer yourself up as a mentor. Our goal when we respond to an emergency scene should be to operate as efficiently as possible. How would it feel to have a crew operate similar to how your right hand and left hand work with each other? There is no traditional communication that takes place; it is referred to as implicit communication. Decision Making Researcher Dr. Gary Klein refers to a samurai solider as an example, if the samurai has to think about what moves he will make with his sword – he's dead, it's too late. However, his mind and hands work without conscious thought and the actions are seamless – a precision reaction. This is a direct result of training our crews and finding out the little items that textbooks and PowerPoints cannot give us. Scott Thompson (2014) provides the Six R's of Training and Experience as a method of assessing the knowledge obtained from training and experience.

- **Recognition** – Basic level and foundation from which knowledge is built. You are able to recognize situations based on your training.

- **Repetition** – The ability to repeat an action. This step demonstrates a level of understanding by the student and the student should be focused on mastering the basic skills.

- **Rehearsal** – The student displays the ability to associate connections between training events/simulations into real world situations.

- **Recital** – This level evaluates the who, what, where, when, how, and to what degree. This step provides the "why" behind what we do.

- **Review** – This is where firefighters maintain their skills. Success is measured by the ability to sustain a high level of performance.

- **Redirection** – This level explicitly demonstrates the ability of the student to read a situation and associate it to previous training and experiences. Based on this past knowledge, skills, and abilities (KSAs) this individual maintains an emphasis on situational awareness, properly applies risk management and crew resource management (CRM) principles and practices (CRM is discussed in detail later).

In his book, Turn the Ship Around, David Marquet describes how he changed the culture, mentality, turn-over rate, and skill level as the commanding officer of his new ship by building the technical competence of his crews. In turn, this also allowed his crews to make more decisions which gave them a sense of fulfillment and accomplishment. This in return allowed the officers to focus on other "stuff" that would help develop the up and comers even more. Being a mentor can be the difference for your people from always being reactive to situations versus being proactive to situations. Building the technical competence covers knowing every piece of your equipment inside and out, capabilities, limitations, alternatives, etc.

Even when the Barn Boss takes the lead on the items mentioned above there will be problems and distractions such as experiencing complacency, taking short-cuts, or having tunnel vision that will occur. The key here is for the Barn Boss to not get sucked into any of these vacuums, but to recognize what is happening and alter it. When this fails to occur, this is where we get hurt. We know not to break glass without gloves, not to break our crew integrity, do not drive through intersections; yet, we still do it. We are our own worst enemy, why do we attempt and find ways to injure or kill ourselves? Is the job not dangerous enough? We have terrorist attacks, HAZ MAT, CBRNE (Chemical, Biological, Radiation, and Nuclear Explosions), plastics, toxic gases, lightweight trusses, etc… Do we really need to add another element to the mix? If we put complacency/short-cuts/lack of education on the list of firefighter injuries and deaths as a cause what would the numbers say? Would it be alarming? Can it all be tied back to leadership?

Do you and your department truly believe in the saying "everyone is a safety officer?" If you are not just providing lip service, do you train everyone to know what to look for? Do you have post-incident critiques? What do you cover in them? If you are an individual, do you take it upon yourself to take in as much knowledge as possible and not just training because you have to? Do you pose questions? Ask for clarification? Do you listen when others speak? No department needs 100 safety officers running around telling firefighters to "tie their shoes" but we do need firefighters and officers that understand building construction components and degradation due to fire, fire behavior in different capacities and fuel loads, and the concept of applying water to name a few.

Company Level Critique

Here is an example of a company level critique that is more specific to the firefighter responsibilities. While these items may be brought up during a full "officer's" critique, sometimes these can be easily overlooked, unless there are specific issues being addressed.

1. Response Time Adequate (Delay issues – train, wrong route, traffic, etc.)
2. Water Supply (Correct lay, adequate GPM, hydrants in working order)
3. 360 conducted

4. Mode of Attack (Was it sufficient?)

5. Hoseline Management

6. Search Operations (Obstacles, timing)

7. RIT (Proper tools / set up)

8. Time from arrival to knockdown (Obstacles, timing)

9. Secondary Search (Was anything found?)

10. Salvage

11. Overhaul

12. Transfer of Command (Was it clear / known?)

12. Any equipment found in disrepair / inoperable?

13. Any other issues to consider that caused concern (Tight space to stretch hose, search difficult due to hoarding, etc…)

14. Preplan available for commercial or street map for subdivision/apartments with correct codes for gates. Hydrant locations marked.

15. Air Management

16. Accountability / crew integrity

If I go back a few years to when I became an instructor for the Gwinnett County Fire and Emergency Services Recruit School, most of the people that I encountered seemed to be more concerned with buying a new toys before graduating recruit school or working all the overtime they could immediately after. While that is not all bad and I have certainly done my share of part time jobs, some of these individuals did not seem to want to take advantage or understand how much of an impact they can have at their level. This is where the informal leader has to step in and show the less experienced firefighters what this job is capable of doing to a person, sometimes even when it is done the right way. We suffer 100,000 injuries and 100 deaths per year (although we have seen a recent decline), not counting the firefighters that do not make it past a year or two out of retirement. We have to start sooner, at the beginning of careers, rather than waiting until later when you are an officer and then try to catch up or make a change. It is too late. Everyone seems preoccupied until something hits them or affects them negatively. We, as a service, have to change this mentality and it starts with the Barn Boss taking the lead. Know your job, Do your job!

Lasky Pride

Part of being the Barn Boss is taking pride and ownership of the tools that belong to you. The tools do not belong to your department, the station, or the public – they purchase, house, and repair, but they are the firefighter's responsibility. You cannot talk about a Barn Boss and not include Pride and Ownership, respectively this section is called Lasky – Pride. There is no better way to state it, however I also consider it part of "Knowing your job and Doing your job." We commonly think about the operations aspect of it, but what about at the station, what about in the community, what about when you're off-duty? Do you ever think of the station as yours? The answer is that everyone should. Every one of us is responsible for our station and with that comes what Retired Fire Chief Rick Lasky has been talking and writing about, "Pride and

Ownership." If you have not read it, then read it. It should be put in every station and put a – real – history book of the fire service and your department, showing your traditions and never forgetting where we came from, in the station as well. One of the lasting impressions I placed on the interviewer when I applied for Gwinnett County was the fact that when she asked me what do you know about GCFES and I recited the history of the department. I told her of its transformation from volunteer to career (1972), where the first station was (Pickneyville), and how many personnel and stations they currently had and I had never lived within two hours of Gwinnett County. However, it meant that much to me to learn where I had set out to start my career. It wasn't just a job interview, it was a career interview. How can one have pride of their history if they do not know their history?

The individual that steps up to the plate, accepts the responsibility of being the Barn Boss, has no problem placing knowledge in the station. The knowledge is not just books either; knowledge is about the sharing of ideas which causes creative destruction. There are times when you have to tear down and rebuild what you may already perceive as great. I have spent numerous amounts of time to provide just something different to my team in order to keep

Station 4 - "Bad Company"

them interested, to keep them thinking about what else is out there past our bays doors. Learning to take pride in your job and being able to say, "Yeah, I work at Station 4, toughest house in the department" – it feels good! As a Barn Boss, it is not about being cocky and it is definitely not about you. One of your primary roles is to set the tone and begin the change factor or improvement of what is already there. Gwinnett County Fire Station #4 was one of the most diverse but most motivated crews that I have ever worked with. This was a trend that was set in place before me; I just brought a new mix to what they already had in motion. The other key role is to help raise that bar and challenge them. People like Driver Engineer Alan Hurd challenged me every day to condition myself for the job, so I accepted the challenge of competing in my first SCOTT Combat Challenge in Tyler, Texas. This in turn challenged him to find new and creative ways to build our strength and conditioning, which usually lasted one – two hours a day with multiple participants from the shift. They saw what was happening and they wanted to be

involved. Every firefighter wants to be a part of something great. We just have to motivate them sometimes to join the ranks. Make it happen, nothing can stop you from being the best you can be. I went on to complete the combat challenge in Tyler,

Scott Combat Challenge Tower – Tyler, Texas 2010

Texas with a time of 3 minutes and 13 seconds. I was able to maintain that same level of training intensity and competed the following year in Charleston, South Carolina. Unfortunately, the time did not change but the time was not important, it was crossing the finish line without stopping. It was the time-spent training with gear acclimation, hands on the tools, and completing an objective without failing. Everything we do should give us pride in our service.

Behavior Modeling and Self Fullfilling Prophecy

One of the items that we discuss in the Training Officers Desk Reference and elaborate on in my Training Officers Boot Camp is Mentoring and Influence. Regardless of what rank you hold, each of us have the ability to mentor. As Lt. General Hal Moore (Mel Gibson) stated in the movie We Were Soldiers, "learn the job above you and teach your job to those below you…" When you begin to

Hose Pack Endurance Training became a daily task.

understand how your influence affects those around you, you will begin to understand how important you are to the core of your crew. One of the stories that I tell is from working in Gwinnett County Station 4 (Truck and Engine Company) as a driver/engineer and these were the days of my acceptance into the Georgia Smoke Diver Program and competing in the Scott Firefighter Combat Challenges. My co-hort Driver/Engineer Alan Hurd (also a retired Ironman competitor) would set up obstacle courses with fire department stuff, gear up, and drill as a daily routine. At first it was just me and him making up "stuff to do." After a while (without forcing, mandating, threatening, etc.,) we had 90% of the entire station (12 personnel) including the lieutenant and captain training with us to some degree. In addition, when we encountered probie firefighters they had no choice but to join us or they would have been exiled on day one. There are two actions that occurred here, 1) is behavior modeling and 2) self-fulfilling prophecy. Both of these are learning and motivational theories at work in this one example. Let's take the behavior modeling theory and discuss it first.

We have all been affected by this in one manner or another whether we realize it or not. The theory states that we will model ourselves after the environment we are placed in. So, if I see someone performing at a high-level of excellence and I recognize it as excellence I will model myself after that environment. However, if I see you sleeping on the couch on truck day and you get away with it I very well may model myself after that as well if I don't know better. As a senior firefighter or officer, a gut check is for you to determine how you are perceived by others. Once the introspection is complete (with your necessary changes) then you can move forward with raising the bar for the minimum expectations of your crew. If I was to tell the guys at station four to gear up without me gearing up first it would not be as effective and no behavior modeling would occur. However, the fact that the others understood what excellence was and wanted to be an active part of it, they invited their selves into the obstacle course punishment. And, when there was a day which I did not feel like setting it up or competing it was the other guys that motivated me to get up. So, it worked both ways – they became as important to me as I was to them.

The second part to discuss is self-fulfilling prophecy. This theory states that what we perceive as reality, is reality. As well, if I perceive excellence as completing the obstacle course every day in turnout gear then that is what I will conform to because I want to be excellent with gear acclimation, dexterity, etc... Case in point, as probie's were assigned to our station they automatically conformed because of how they perceived excellence – they knew no other way. Their minds had not been given the chance to be corrupted.

As senior firefighters, company officers, or training officers – you have the chance to establish what excellence is and what you consider the minimum standard. When you do this several things occur, including teamwork, comradery, and improved knowledge and skills for all. It also creates a level of motivation and buy-in regardless of any generational differences (our age range at station 4 went from 24 to 50). By setting this example, you are mentoring those around you and establishing the next generation of the fire service. Great friend and one of my mentors, Joey Hartley (actually one of my first instructors at the state fire academy) asked in a recent article – "Will you pick up the torch and move it forward?" As experience leaves every day from our industry, we need people to take the reins and lead us into the next phase.

Try this food for thought from the Civil War Era:

In the book, Robert E. Lee on Leadership, one of his deciding factors in promoting an individual was how well their camp was kept. He figured that if a soldier could keep a clean and organized camp then they would be efficient and organized on the battlefield. The same theory can apply to the Fire Service. It is a unique concept that the orderliness of your camp area could play a large role in your effectiveness as an officer. I tend to agree with this theory, if there is no regard for the station or your camp... Will there be any regard for your gear, the truck, or your tools? Do you know without a doubt that when you pull the rope on the saw it will work when you need it on the fire ground? Something as simple as this attention to detail will show what kind of leader you are. In addition, these are items that company officers should have no involvement in, it's not their job. If I did not have to see my company officers, I did my job for the day. The best damn firefighter is nothing more than playing dress up without his or her tools. If a tool was needed to get you out of a trapped situation do you make it out alive or not? Finish your own story...

Knowing your job, doing your job, having pride, understanding behavior modeling and skill mastery, these are all points that the Barn Boss needs to possess. This is who the Barn Boss is; the rest of this book will further discuss characteristics and specific jobs of the Barn Boss.

Barn Bosses need training materials and to know that you do not have to reinvent the wheel. Here is a sample of training article from July 2016 Fire Engineering Magazine:

Developing Tactical Decision Games

The Gambler's Fallacy is described as believing that luck will eventually come or just this once you can beat the odds. In order to illustrate this concept in my officer development classes I randomly select a student and ask them to pick a number and then I hand them dice and tell them to roll the number. Do you know people in your department that use this very same method on the incident scene? Regardless if it is their fault from a lack of training or due to a lack of experience – the outcome can unfortunately be the same if they are not lucky. The key here is understanding how to bridge this gap through building experiences on the incident scene and through effective training. One proven method of building this experience is through the use of tactical decision games.

Dr. Gary Klein coined Tactical Decisions Games (TDGs) after researching for the military on how to provide realistic training without the possibility of losing lives (using real bullets) or taxing resources (expensive). Dr. Klein decided to spend time with multiple fire departments due to the similarities between the battlefield and the fire ground. The fire ground also provided a high enough frequency of events where he could actually review the decisions made and then interview the incident commander afterwards to determine how they developed their actions. After years of studying these decisions in the actual field, good and bad, he was able to develop a framework for training soldiers in low hazard environments with highly effective training retention. The term Recognition Primed Decision Making was born out of this same research and was a driving factor behind the TDGs.

Physical Fidelity is constructing a prop or simulation to the exact replica of the actual environment. Consider the environment of conducting a live fire drill or a pilot in a highly realistic cockpit simulator.

Psychological Fidelity is constructing a drill that uses the brainpower more so than muscles, however, they can be integrated to work within the same drills. Here you will see where mental stressors are included in the training, such as time limits.

It is also very important to consider how our brains function as a novice and as an expert. Generally, novices usually work off the Law of Association, "this means that" or they associate items as relating to one another. Checklists are generally used by the novice and provide guidance. The expert uses cues and clues to determine the correct strategy or tactic. As well, they may have the same checklist as the novice however they do not rely on it – it is only a reference. The major difference, which is very much based on experiences, is that when the situation turns to something different from what is on the checklist the expert understands or has a "Gut Instinct" in what decision to make next. The novice may stumble at this point; however, there is hope for building everyone's experiences while waiting for the next call.

General Colin Powell has been quoted as using the 40-70 rule. If he did not have 40% of the information, he did not have enough information to make a good decision. However, if he had more than 70% of the information the chance to strike has passed him by. In fire service terms, if you do not have enough information or knowledge to make the decision – we get someone hurt or lose control (not seeing the big picture or freelancing). Once the house burns down, you have 100% of the information you need and it is too late to act. The best decision in the world will not rebuild it. This is also referred to as the Goldilocks Effect, too cold and too hot = too little and too much information. This causes us to be indecisive and miss opportunities to make a difference.

In my officer development classes, I break the Tactical Decision Games (TDGs) into five different formats. The very first one is free (no cost) and simple compared to the last one, which has a cost and takes time to develop. Below I will briefly describe these formats and how they can be applied in the station and at the fire academy. In the actual training session, we walk through a matrix which helps you decide on what to train for along with determining the audience, and critical factors involved. This process helps the facilitator to provide a focused training path.

In this section, we also discuss the importance of time as a stress factor. Other stress factors that can be used include using turnout coat and helmet, wearing an SCBA, and using a radio. As for the facilitator, the role-playing activity is very much in effect for these exercises. A script should be developed with questions and benchmarks and the facilitator should be quick on his or her feet – always staying one-step ahead of the student and thinking in multiple directions. Thinking in multiple directions means considering all of the possible avenues the student could take to mitigate the incident and having a response for the student's response. The multi-pronged approach allows students/firefighters to be actively involved in the training and the facilitator provides a positive critique of decisions to build off of.

Dr. Gary Klein developed the following model for the recognition primed decision making process:

1. Diagnose the Situation (Size-Up)

2. Is situation typical? (What is the relevant information?)

3. Recognition of cues, clues, and expectancies

4. Mental Simulation (Evaluate your actions mentally – will your action do what it is supposed to?)

5. Make a decision

6. Implement course of action

7. Evaluate actions

8. Repeat

#2 – The One Page Lesson

This is simply what it says, it is one page with an incident photo and a few questions. Fire Engineering and I have teamed up to provide a one-page lesson every two weeks on their website under the Training Officer's Toolbox. While this is a no cost item, it does take time to locate good pictures and develop  answers for the post training critique. The facilitator places the paper face down in front of the firefighter and tells them they have 30, 60, or 90 seconds to review the photo and answer the questions. The time depends on the complexity of the scenario and the Knowledge, Skills and Abilities (KSA) of the audience. This is also an excellent format to practice/discuss situational awareness which I see as three items – 1) Identify the issue, 2) Comprehend what it is, and 3) Predict what is going to happen. In this example, the facilitator only acts as the timekeeper and reviews the key points of the exercise. In class, I ask the students to discuss their answers so that we can learn from each other and see if other answers agree or disagree. This is an excellent tool to use for training instead of using a PowerPoint to cover the same information. www.FireServiceSLT.com provides multiple (and free) One Page Lessons/TDGs. In this particular TDG the students had 60 seconds to read and answer three questions. The three questions include:

1. What is your first priority stepping off Engine Co.?
2. What assignment are you giving to your Driver and FF?
3. What is survivability of occupants?

#3 – Go to the Whiteboard

In this TDG, I have the firefighters look in the opposite direction while I draw the structure layout and landmarks (hydrants, streets, etc..). Once the drawing is complete, I provide a dispatch

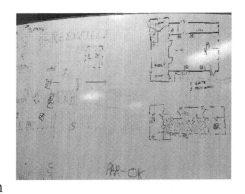

to the firefighter and allow them 20 – 30 seconds to ask questions before I allow them to turn around. Once they turn around it is "real time," the firefighter is on scene with other apparatus/staffing on the way (this should be based on current department resources). The student should provide a size up and start running through whichever acronym the department uses (SLICE-RS, RECEO-VS, COAL WAS WEALTH, ETC.). As units/resources begin to arrive, which is usually about every 30 seconds, this keeps the stress level up and the firefighter must respond with an assignment. The facilitator must keep up with all assignments/re-assignments because it is vital in the critique to determine if the "incident commander" kept up with his/her resources. Now, in order to make this TDG successful, you must pre-write an objective for the training – what are you trying to accomplish, develop a dispatch, script, timeline, base it on current resources and judge your audience (the 30 seconds mentioned earlier could be 15 for the expert or 45 for the beginner). Students could be asked to use two-way radios or wear turnout gear in order to add realism and stress.

#4 – Walk-Around

The Walk-Around has a very similar approach to the #3 – White Board; however, this one requires a four-sided view of the structure, which can be done in two ways. The first is simply to take photos of structures in your first-in or to take a video of you walking around the structure so that it is real time and the student feels that unknown effect (adding stress) as he/she is viewing on an overhead screen. One unique approach is to have a split screen between what the eye sees and what a thermal imaging camera detects – very effective. The stress level went up as now the student has even more to pay attention too. I use a simple PowerPoint presentation with embedded videos to produce this training. Finding 4-sided views of structures with actual smoke showing also adds an extreme amount of realism. The same rules apply here as in #3. Once the first slide is displayed, I provide a dispatch to the firefighter and other apparatus/staffing are on the way (this should be based on current department resources). The student should provide a size up and start running through whichever acronym the department uses (SLICE-RS, RECEO-VS, COAL WAS WEALTH, ETC.). As units/resources begin to arrive, which is usually about every 30 seconds, this keeps the stress level up and the firefighter must respond with an assignment. The facilitator must keep up with all assignments/re-assignments because it is vital that in the critique that it is determined if the "incident commander" kept up with his/her resources the same principles apply for the objective of the training, develop a dispatch, script, timeline, base it on current resources and know your audience. Students could be asked to use two-way radios or wear turnout gear in order to add realism and stress. The benefit to this format is that it can be completely packaged and ready to go well before training day and saved. All of the others take some development the day of the class.

#5 – Active Simulation

Up to this point, everything has been no cost or minimum expense for the Fire Engineering Magazine (which provides other information not associated with the actual training we are discussing here – two birds with one stone). For the active simulation, I use Digital Combustion – Fire Studio Software, which provides numerous options for developing stress on participants. In the grand scheme – for most organizations this is a small cost, which you can use repeatedly over time at no additional cost. All of the same rules and principles apply here as they did in #3 and #4 so I will not take up additional space. However, the facilitator's role becomes much more difficult as they are responsible for building the simulation using pre-loaded pictures or ones that you have taken and up loaded. This individual does need to have some tech-savvy to assist in speeding up the learning curve for building simulations. The "extra benefits" here is that it allows you to add additional realism such as sound, video, smoke and fire movement. The facilitator can also add options in case the student/firefighter makes a decision to vent a window or if a firefighter ambiguously assigns a crew ventilation with no specific direction – I have a slide option for this specific scenario.

The key in all of these simulations is to place stress on the student using the Tactical Decision Game approach, without creating hazards and reducing training cost. There will never be a replacement for live / hands-on training however, this type of training will provide slide trays and experiences for the firefighter and officer to draw from as proven by Dr. Gary Klein and Dr.

Gasaway. Steven Mills (2014) stated in his Sizing Up the Fireground Leader article that "advanced exposure to potential situations through actual incidents, a review of past incidents, training, self-study, or any combination of these items provides essential information fireground leaders can reference during an initial and continuous fireground size-up." As officers at your respective stations, I challenge you to study the research, learn how to develop meaningful training and then put it to good use.

An example of a TDG which can be used today has been provided here on the next page.

Tactical Decision Game

You have three minutes to read the statement and answer the questions below in order of highest priority.

You are the Lt. assigned to E10. E10 is dispatched to a reported structure fire in CO. 14's first-in district. The fire is located in a Restaurant. The fire building consists of a large one story, Type II, commercial building. The fire is located on Side D of the building. E14, E26 and E21 are conducting fire attack operations inside the building. Battalion 3 is the IC and assigns E10 rapid intervention group responsibilities. Your crew consists of a 4 year firefighter, a 5 year relief driver and yourself.

What equipment will you need?
What verbal communications will you give to your crew?
What radio channels will your crew monitor?
What are your responsibilities as a RIT Group Leader?

Key Points

- Leadership is more than just an age or rank. It's what you do with your age and rank; regardless if you're a 24 year old firefighter or a 40 year old captain.
- Know your Job, Do your Job.
- Remember the power of influence.
- Make it a priority to learn the new trends, do the core competencies and learn something new every day.
- Don't be afraid to have goals and finish through. If you want it, go accomplish it.
- Take pride in your station, equipment, and tools. Read "Pride and Ownership," Chief Rick Lasky.
- Remember Robert E. Lee's factor for deciding a promotion. A clean and organized camp will help you achieve that promotion.
- Most importantly, finish your own story… Be the Barn Boss!

Chapter 2

"The art of leadership lies in simple things – commonsense actions that ensure high moral and increase the odds of winning."

Retired United States Navy Captain Michael Ashbroft

Sources of Power

The Sources of Power title comes from two different backgrounds. The first is Gary Klein's Sources of Power and trusting your intuition. As we build our knowledge and skill levels our ability to make decisions improves. As well, it develops our ability to garner respect from those around you for the knowledge and skills that you possess. The second aspect of this chapter title comes from Shierberg and Shierberg describing the Social Power and Influence Model. They use a model developed in 1962 by John French and Bertram Raven which depicts six different forms of power. These forms of power are Expert, Referent, Legitimate, Reward, Coercive and Informational Power. We will discuss these topics and explain how to set the tone with your crew.

"As we build our knowledge and skill levels our ability to make the correct decision improves."

Expert – Expert power is derived from the knowledge and skills developed through various means, generally speaking it combines the cognitive and psychomotor functions. The individual with the expert power understands the field struggles in addition to understanding the science behind what is occurring. In most cases, having just the cognitive or just the psychomotor skill does not constitute being an expert. The true expert is the individual who can not only perform the task but truly understands what is occurring beyond what the eye is seeing. Generally, individuals with a high level of competency in both skills sets are progressive types with a desire to be a lifelong student of their craft. They are a motivated breed and lead the way in many cases because they think for themselves. They are willing to be mavericks to some degree but not to the point of freelancing or at the cost of another individual. Colonel John Boyd was considered a maverick fighter pilot. However, he became highly recognized for his development of the OODA Loop (Orient, Observe, Decide, Act) thought process which was designed to sharpen the decision making capabilities of Air Force fighter pilots. This concept can now be found in many arenas including John Salka's "First In, Last Out" discussing leadership in the Fire Department of New York City. Chet Richards, a close friend of John Boyd, publicized the OODA Loop concept in his "Certain to Win" book which describes the application in a business and military setting.

As you will read later in this chapter, David Marquet describes this as technical competence and requires your peers to be experts of their functions. By your peers being experts you are able to delegate task and move past the simple easily seen issues and face more complex or in-depth concerns because everyone is on the same page. As well, when the time comes for succession planning there is a clear path and when you take a day off, your crew operates flawlessly.

Referent – Referent power is based on the relationships and personality of an individual. Typically, at the fire station there was always someone, generally the driver/engineer (or Barn Boss), behind the scenes that was making everything happen without the formal officer persuasion. This position built their credibility due to their knowledge, skills, abilities demonstrated and their personality without a formal rank. I believe this also gives itself to the expectancy theory where people will rise to what they perceive as the expectation of great.

If you type in your internet search "Leadership Lessons from the Dancing Guy" you will find an odd video where one man starts dancing to his own beat. While some of us may see this as strange and possibly look the other way, some of us may find it intriguing and feel a desire to belong to something freely. It begins with one individual joining, then two, then ten and then hundreds join the dancing group due to one guy doing what he believes. There were no threats, formal ranking, coerciveness, and he surely was not an expert dancer. This was about people joining something they felt was larger than themselves. In many cases people with referent power have brought many groups together for good and bad reasons. The key as an outsider looking in is to be sure that virtues and values of these leaders are in the right place.

Legitimate – Legitimate power is described as a formal ranking from within an organization. Growing up, in the career sense, in the fire department which is a para-military structure the source of Legitimate Power is very prominent. There is a rank and file of individuals based on promotional testing, work history, interviews, and past work related incidents. In the situation of a fire incident or a military battle there is very little time to wait for someone to step up and be a leader. Decisions must be made in a decisive manner in order to ensure firefighters go home and citizen's lives are protected. Without a formal leader in place sometimes situations reach a failure stage that cannot be reversed. However, just as there are issues with all models of power, the problem here may be hidden through the testing processes or absences thereof, the Good Ol' Boy system, etc… The pure presence of legitimate power does not make you a great leader.

Reward – Reward power is based on the individual who may be able to offer unique experiences, bonuses, employment opportunities, praises, and enthusiasm. At first, your thoughts are directly tied to your place of employment, however with this type of power you may be considering your networking abilities and the people who you work with outside of your employment place. For example, within the International Society of Fire Service Instructors, this organization is in the truest sense a member driven organization that has seen numerous accomplishments from volunteers. There is not one member who receives financial incentives for the work produced; however, they realize the opportunities and experiences to be a part of something larger than one's own self. This organization can provide a network of individuals where all of your questions can be answered. This organization has the respect and ability to navigate the national service and offer qualified members the chance to start a teaching career, attend AFG Panelist Reviews, work with NIST and UL, and write books such as the Training Officer's Desk Reference with Jones and Bartlett. All of these items are rewards from a non-profit organization – they have reward power. If you are in a position to formally recognize employees for a good job, do it. If you are not in a formal position, you can still recognize employees for a job well done. It may have come from a tough call, a good knockdown, a save – recognition in front of just the station crew is the responsibility of the Barn Boss. The Barn Bosses job is to make sure this happens.

Coercive – Coercive power is described as forcing someone to comply through various means such as threats of physical, psychological, and emotional consequences. This style aligns with the old school "Iron Fist Mentality." While this may provide short term success, it will never see long term success and generally shows weakness of the leader as having hidden deficiencies. This does not mean that you cannot hold people accountable formally and informally. It simply means that you need to set expectations, work to develop your peers/employees, provide constructive feedback on failures, and treat your crew as a family.

As you review the sources of power described above and think through Gary Klein's development of your ability to make decisive decisions, you must understand how to be engaged. You must be engaged to the point where your commitment is not that of the egg but that of bacon. Think about your engagement in the terms of stocks. Just like in the stock market we have to know when to buy stock and how to buy stock – it requires you to be engaged. Being engaged is extremely important in our profession, probably more so in the Fire/EMS profession than any other profession. This is just for the simple fact that a majority of our decisions deal with life and death. Firefighting is not just a job; it is a way of life. You do not become a firefighter, firefighting becomes you. Yes, it is an old cliché but it is true. What I am talking about is the fact that anyone can get a certificate, anyone can get a job with the Title Firefighter, I've seen them come and I've seen them go. However, when you love what you do it is not the title you care or even think about. It becomes the things that you do to try to make a difference for the good of the company and the service that you deliver to the internal and external customers. Once you have done that, you have bought stock into what it means to be a firefighter and hopefully it is stock that you will keep forever.

Cultivating Sources of Power

When we think about cultivating sources of power the first place we should look is within our team or station. This is where it all starts, really the –Meat and Potatoes - of the entire concept. Simple enough, you did not need this book to tell you that, most of you already know that. So, why am I writing about sources of power if it is so simple? Well, I am about to tell you!

In the last chapter, we talked about 'Knowing your Job, Doing your Job," so you know and do your job, but do you believe in what you do, in everything that you do? Do you believe that the manner in which you pay particular attention to every detail when checking out the truck in the morning matters? How about just cleaning the bay floors every night? Buying stock is so much more than just knowing and doing; it is believing that it's the right thing to do and that even cleaning the floors can make a difference. We spoke earlier about the Self Fullfilling Prophecy Theory and that what we perceive as reality is reality, perception is reality. Buying stock is going above and beyond the call of duty to change someone's life. Maybe you spend extra time making sure your truck is top notch, your station does not have a spec of dirt, or maybe you train just because you have the time to and not because you have to. I have known several engineers that were so particular about their trucks that they would not be caught putting a brush on the paint, they hand washed it because of the harm the brush may do to the paint. If they're taking that much time on their truck, I am willing to bet that every piece of equipment on that truck received the same amount of care. On a fire scene, that's the truck I want to pull equipment off of to use. They get it! Barn Bosses should instill this mentality into their crew using the correct sources of power.

Setting the Tone Early

Ask yourself these questions. When someone new comes in the station do you take the time to explain expectations, and ask for their input? Do you let them know that this is a team, it is our station and we are going to make it the best station there is? The paint may be chipped, there may be bare spots of grass out front, there may even be leaks in the roof, but your name is tied to that station. It is either a good name and it can be trusted, or it's a smudged name and nobody wants to be associated with it. Your reputation will always precede you; keep that in the back of your mind.

You may not know everyone's name at your department and definitely not in the Fire Service as a whole; but if I was from the most disciplined and busiest house in the department would you have a different respect or impression of me versus a slower house or one that always causes trouble? I remember a particular freckled red-headed (there is only one of you – Chief), not even close to being politically correct, captain (at the time) that had a crew that would follow him anywhere and it was known throughout the department. If someone walks up to you and says I am from Rescue 3, without even saying a department, what is your first thought? Mine is FDNY, their known for being a hell of a company and tested frequently. Spending some time with one of the products of FDNY and Rescue 3, Retired Chief John Norman, I would be willing to bet that the firefighters at Rescue 3 have bought stock in their station and what they do every day. Obviously, not every station has the name recognition worldwide that they have but why not let it be known that

2009 Gwinnett County Leadership and Safety Conference (L – R) – Clinton Crites, John Norman, and Jug

your station is the best in your department or the state. However, do not take just your own word for it when you think you are doing a good job. It comes from when people stop you to say, "I looked all around this area and your department really stood out to me." When others voluntarily put in transfers to your station just to be a part of your team, this is when you know.

Many times it is the little things that matter, sometimes minimum cost or effort involved. I recently presented my department with the organization's first challenge coin. In the private sector they are not accustomed to many of the fire service and military traditions so I explained to them the  history of the coin and what it means to possess the coin. I preceded to share my vision of our department – what it was and what it could be and I asked them if they accepted? They accepted the vision and every time they look at the coin it is a reminder of what excellence is. They amaze me every day and I am grateful to be a part of such a great team (the cost was $600 and the coin will last a life time). Other times, it is as simple as spending $20 and providing sports drinks to the crews for no other reason than working and training. They remember and appreciate these things.

Best Damn Station in the Department

"Rockin the Ville Since '81"
Station 15

How do you present yourself when you are at work? One day my operations chief and I were watching our on-duty crew walk through our facility on their way to a training drill location and noticed that they were spread out, in smaller groups, with one or two people handling all of the equipment. They seemed very discombobulated and resembled nothing that a team should look like. We allowed the crew to make it to the training drill and start setting up. What we noticed next was that even after making it to the training drill the team continued in their smaller groups and each group seemed to want to do their own thing. Before the end of the training, the team started to become frustrated due to the fact that stuff wasn't coming together like it was supposed to and some had words for each other before it was all said and done. The next day my operations chief and I discussed what we saw, our concerns and laid out a plan to address.

During the next training event I asked the crew to spread out the equipment evenly amongst each other and walk tightly together, as one group. We were conducting a social experiment from within the facility and we needed their assistance. So, they worked as one team and walked two by two all the way through the facility. If I think back to my double house days were we would respond an engine, truck, and med unit to an incident with lights beaming and sirens blaring – the excitement, the adrenaline, the coolness of $2 million dollars barreling down Peachtree Corners and Downtown Lawrenceville. This is the same feeling this crew started to feel due to the fact that everyone in the facility noticed them. Other employees stopped doing their jobs just to look up and see what was going on. On the way back from the training, non-emergency operational employees were stopping our crew and asking how they could be part of the team. Once we returned my operations chief asked the team if they had felt anything different and every one of them felt the change. Learning points – you don't have to criticize someone to make a point, perception is reality, and let people think solutions are their own ideas.

Another book, if you have not read it, you should – "Management Techniques for the Best Damn Ship in the Navy," by Captain Michael Abrashoff. When Captain Abrashoff took over command of the USS Benfold, it was known as one of the worst ships in the fleet, the moral was low and the sailors couldn't wait to jump ship or get out of the Navy all together. In addition to the obstacles he was facing, he was the junior officer in the fleet. With all of that on him, within two years the USS Benfold did a 180 degree turn around and was taking every award the fleet offered, surpassing all of the other ships in everything imaginable. How could he do such a thing? He was the junior officer of the fleet but the Fleet Commander started looking to him for recommendations and he knew he could count on Captain Abrashoff when a job needed to be taken care of. He was able to get his crew to buy stock in the ship and over time, a relatively short period of time, they started to understand what it meant to be the Best Damn Ship in the Navy. How about making your station the Best Damn Station in the Department, Region, and State by applying the appropriate sources of power. Captian Abrashoff worked for his employees and not the other way around. The possibilities are endless to what an effective Barn Boss can accomplish.

Heart!!!

It's referred to as the 80/10/10 Rule and it is in every department and organization. 80% of your team gets it – they train, study, mentor, etc… 10% of your team is on the fence – they just need a little help and someone to show them the way. The last 10% of your team is past the point of return.

There is also the Pareto Rule – it says you will spend 80% of your time dealing with those last 20%. Those in the 80% range want to be at the busy station, the disciplined station, they have the desire and they are bought in. On occasions, there are some that need a little help in making the right choices and that is where we tie in the Barn Boss again, in leading the firefighters to the right stock. And that's ok if they need some help from time to time, as long as you have an individual that has their heart in the right spot, you can do anything with that. We all need help or a little guidance from time to time, do not abandon folks if they slip or make a mistake – learn from it and build them up. People tend to underestimate how much heart really means in the Fire Service. Quite frankly, I would take heart over brains and muscle any day, because that person with the heart will accomplish ten times as much as either of the others due to shear desire and determination. We can teach the knowledge and build the muscles, you cannot give someone heart. They have to show it.

I had the privilege of being a Recruit School Instructor before transferring to the Career Development Division within training. One of the key things that I miss is watching someone that may not be the top physical specimen or score the top grade on every test but they were consistent and you knew they would never give up because that meant defeat and that was not acceptable to them. They had HEART, and lots of it. This is what we need in the Fire Service, because these are the individuals that are going to buy stock into the program and make it great. Moreover, if your station is already great they will make it that much better.

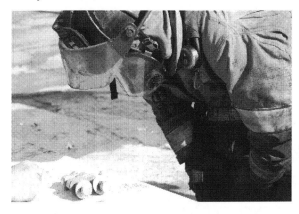

Nuts and Bolts Drill on Day 6 of GSD

One of the programs in Georgia that exemplified this for me personally is the Georgia Smoke Diver Program where I had to gut check my own heart level as I went through the toughest training program I had ever witnessed. However, coming out the other side successfully was the greatest feeling imaginable and drives you to be that much better. I went through this program in November of 2009, however I started training (mentally and physically) months earlier. I completed the qualification test, was accepted to the program and then competed in the grueling program. There was a discipline, a sense of pride and a commitment to go beyond the station walls. As "Smoke Daddy" and City of Atlanta Battalion Chief David Rhodes stated, the course probably didn't teach you very many new skills but it perfected your ability to perform your skills under stress. Retired Captain L. David Marquet, in his book *Turn the Ship Around,* calls this technical competency. Creating technical competency in your crew members will develop confidence in their decision making and give them the ability to challenge others around them, Technical Competency = Expert Power. I encourage you to read some of Dr. Gary Klein's decision making research as well. His work covers many different applications, including the fire service, and discusses how to design training under stress to assist in building your experience.

Just like the stock market when you invest you want a return (ROI – Return on Investment). You want to make sound financial moves, so hopefully you can buy that new car, house or maybe just retire with no worries. I like a return every once in a while, that is human. It is the same principle as the stock market, but it is what you expect to get in return that is the difference. You have to look long term just like in the stock market, this quarter it may be down but if you look at it over the last 5 or 10 years it may have went up 6% to 10%. Stock in the station is the same thing; do not expect pats on the back or touchy feely letters from your company officer. It will pay off when promotions come up and the chief officers are looking for an individual that can be trusted whom they know will work hard, handle their business and work just that much harder because they appreciate the recognition of being promoted. The individual did the job year after year, they were consistent, they have a purpose, and they promote a mentality that is pertinent to success. They went above and beyond, and volunteered for the hard assignments, and then succeeded when the cards were stacked against them.

Diversifying

Let us move on to being engaged outside of your department, we are going to diversify. What does buying outside stock mean? Buying into programs such as Everyone Goes Home, become an Advocate for safety, work with the National Fallen Firefighters Foundation, ISFSI (International Society of Fire Service Instructors); you can even develop your own program(s). Still, what does all of this mean?

"Is knowledge really power?"

Ask yourself, "Is knowledge really power?" The answer is yes, so why not learn it and share it. Every firefighter has encountered different situations at different times, sometimes their choices worked and sometimes they did not. We have to learn from these, the Near Miss Program and Firefighter Close Calls examine all kinds of situations that deal with individuals getting hurt or performing in a way that almost hurt someone. Learn the new techniques and methods, if it works – promote it. Recently, many people have argued against the fire related research of Underwriters Laboratory and National Institute of Standards and Technology. Why? A sound firefighter is a firefighter that understands both sides of the story, and can apply the appropriate action for the appropriate situation. In a combat situation we should bring all available knowledge to the battle ground.

One of the smartest moves that I made was to invest my time in the Everyone Goes Home Program (EGH) and the International Society of Fire Service Instructors Society (ISFSI). The benefits were two fold. The first was the knowledge that I gained and the mentors that I found that greatly influenced my career. The second is the knowledge, information and opportunities that I was able to bring back to my department and station. It created opportunities that other stations and departments have to work for or incur some kind of cost in order to receive. The networking opportunities are second to none and the mentors I gained throughout my career could never be repaid.

If you come up with your own excellent idea put it out there for people to take something away from it. Gwinnett County Fire and Emergency Services does this; if an individual has an idea they fill out a form and take the idea to the Research and Development (R & D) Committee to show what it can do for their department. In my next department a few years later, I created the Innovation

Committee where any employee could document and submit an idea and this reached beyond just the emergency operations and found its way into the business side of our organization. The R & D and Innovation committees are made up of field personnel that understand the struggles everyone is going through and are constantly looking for innovations. A lot of good ideals and practices have come from this approach. There can be nothing more gratifying than putting material out there that saved someone from injury or death. Just one person, just one time; and then whatever it took I know it was damn well worth it. The trick that you have to remember though is that you will not always see this. If nobody is getting hurt or incidents are not happening, you may never know that you made a difference until you look at the big picture. Through the EGH program and being a Train-the-Trainer for the Courage to be Safe program, I have been able to teach all across Georgia for free. I have spent a lot of time away from home and invested a generous amount of my own money into providing the program. However, I may never know what the outcomes are of most of these departments or what could potentially have happened without the discussion, but I would like to think that someday – somewhere, something that I said made a difference in just one firefighter. Then, it was all worth all.

Look at some of the big names in the Fire Service. How did they get there? How many lives have they touched? How many situations could have been different if knowledge was not shared? Retired FDNY Deputy Chief John Norman made one of the greatest lasting impressions on me years ago in Cobb County, Georgia while teaching a strategy and tactics class. In the last slide or two of his presentation, he put up a picture of his son, a FDNY Firefighter, riding the same truck that Chief Norman rode as a company officer. I cannot quite quote what he said exactly, but I understood the message and remember the concept well. If you have the knowledge get it out there, it may just save someone's life and think about how would you live everyday if you knew that there is something that you could have done to make a difference in an injury or death. If you do not have the knowledge, then find it and then find someone to share it with. It may just be your family riding in that seat one day. The conviction with which he said it left an imprint on me, I knew at that point, that is a trait I want to model.

This is what I am talking about, buying stock outside of your department, do something that will save people's lives – Make A Difference. As far as I am concerned there can never be too many learning programs, as long as everybody is doing something in one of them. Every firefighter has a different experience and situation that they have faced or learned from; put it out there for everyone to see. It is another avenue to share information and open people's eyes.

The Power of not being Mr. Popular

As we begin to understand the various sources of power and how they apply to a given circumstance we may not always be the most popular. I will say that being engaged is not always the most popular option; people will have jokes and ridicule you at times. Just as Dan Madrzykowski and Steve Kerber were leaders in the new fire science studies they took several blows but never backed down from their research that is ultimately making us better. The ISFSI also saw its fair share of nay-sayers however, thousands of people across the country attended their Principles of Modern Fire Attack Course and a thousand more joined the organization.

Never listen to the naysayers because some day you or something that you put together will make a difference (or, they could never do what you were doing to begin with and it makes them feel inferior). One of my bosses while I was in the training division, Assistant Chief Greg Schaffer said, "People don't throw daggers at the individuals behind them, they throw daggers at the people out front leading." Think about how true this statement is.

You may be familiar with the program Everyone Goes Home and their class, "Courage to be Safe". Doing what is right within an organization will not always make you the most popular individual. Sometimes it is hard to have the Courage to be Safe, to stand up when it is needed, and buy into something bigger than any one person or object. If you have the courage, then lead - if you don't, then learn how too.

Demonstrator of Beliefs

As we have walked through what it takes to be a Barn Boss, think about the individual that says one thing and then does the exact opposite. Or, maybe you've seen the person that has the do as I say, not as I do mentality. These types of individuals are not demonstrators of their beliefs, they stand for nothing. A large majority of these are the individuals that are looking out for themselves at that moment but not looking at the long-term consequences of their actions. Always remember, the piper gets paid eventually. In the short term, as people begin to observe the grand scheme of these types of individuals, their credibility begins to slip away. Once your credibility is lost, it is nearly impossible to regain that respect back. Study the sources of power and how to apply the various types for the right reasons.

Having the Passion

"A great leader's courage to fulfill his vision comes from passion, not position." John Maxwell

When you find that topic or subject that drives you and you're passionate about it, then stand up for it. Whether you are a firefighter or a chief officer, when your passion comes from the heart, it carries a hundred times more of an impact – it is the conviction within the message. If you will allow your brain to decipher the difference between the trivial and essential items, and then allow your heart to guide and drive your passion for these items, you will accomplish a tremendous amount of

work. This passion is not something that an individual can fake or attempt to have. You either have it or not, and it is up to you to obtain it, if you want it. People, especially firefighters, can read what an individual is truly saying by their body language and demeanor. I specifically talk about this in the Training Officers Desk Reference where we discuss the traits of an instructor and the importance of detail from the gig line to the shine on the boots. A training officers first shot at credibility comes from their appearance, if this is true, then it equally applies to every informal leader on the floor performing the job.

Now, with having this passion you have to learn to be smart about it. There are some individuals that attempt to force their opinions and thoughts upon the audience. You want to try to persuade these individuals while not forcing your thoughts upon them. The ability of someone to accept a concept or to change their behavior is much easier to obtain when it is a joint effort. This joint effort comes from that particular point when the audience understands and accepts your point-of-view as credible. Then, the audience has to make the commitment to change their own behavior individually. It is really as simple as if you come up with the idea on your own and it's a good idea you are going to use it. Your goal should be to use this same delivery method and allow your audience to develop their own idea based on your point-of-view. You will gain more acceptances through this type of delivery than slamming your fist down or yelling – the iron fist mentality which has prevailed in many industries for many years. It is also important to remember to be respectful and acknowledge others opinions and ideas. Part of your passion should be listening to what they are saying, they may be able to provide an insight that you did not think about or consider.

Choose your Battles Wisely

As with any topic, there will always be individuals that are in opposition. As well, there are some topics that are not as important as others – this is where learning prioritization is important. One example of this is an individual that makes a stand on topics that are small, minute, non-safety related items and neglect items such as training, crew integrity, and safety. However, they chose to make a stand because they believe in it. If it is that much of a passionate item for you, then by all means. However, be aware that you may be using your energy on items that will not have a great positive impact, instead of using your energy on the people that matter, the firefighters, your crew. The concept of this last sentence is also known as servant leadership. Take care of the people that are taking care of you. Consider your battles within your team, as the saying goes - your crew can make you or break you.

Once you choose to pick a battle, know your subject inside and out. Research every aspect of the subject; know where to find resources to support your idea. What do others in different regions have to say about it? Look for models of where your idea has worked before, maybe in a different part of the country. Similar to when you give a presentation to any panel, look at the positive and negative, and question your idea. Find the weak areas and anticipate what questions you may be asked. Use these questions to prepare yourself and answer these questions before the audience is allowed the chance to ask these questions. Basically, you do not want to show up to a gun fight with a knife. Once you have prepared yourself by researching and studying the subject, show a level of confidence when presenting. Speak clearly and boldly, with decisiveness, and most of all remain calm. The ISFSI used this very approach when developing the Principles of Modern Fire Behavior based on the research and science provided by UL and NIST.

As an example, I was asked to prepare a presentation for the need of an updated Fast Track Program for experienced and previously certified new hires. I was the lead instructor for this program and understood the ins and outs of the program. As well, I understood the reasons for the program and where the program originated. I researched similar programs within other departments and reviewed training injuries and line-of-duty-deaths tirelessly. I was proposing that the requirements be kept to a very high standard since they were being allowed to bypass the traditional 13 week fire recruit school. Using case studies and reviewing the history of similar programs, this provided me with the background information that I needed. In the end, very few questions were presented mainly because the challenges were confronted head on.

Now, even with the best preparation and everything outlined perfectly, you may not always get the support that you are anticipating. There have been various issues such as staffing, financial, and workload issues that have kept great proposals from moving forward. Some of the greatest ideas have been put in a folder and placed on a shelf. Eventually, it will come back around and when it does you will be ready for it. The time in-between may even allow you to provide additional information or alter the program to better fit within the realm of its needs. Conducting a true needs assessment for your crew will assist you in determining the difference between "need to have" and "nice to have."

No Questions can be Good Questions

During the beginning of my tenor as a training officer, I was asked to prepare a presentation for the Incident Safety Officer Program that would be implemented in the coming months for new and current officers. As I was one of the first to work on the program, Captain Wayne Mooney (now Deputy Chief) kept me attached to the program and allowed me to become the face of it early on. This was the first time that I had stood in front of the entire

command staff including all of the battalion and deputy chiefs together. Nervousness does not come close to explaining how I felt. I prepared my 20-minute presentation and

Dan Hansen, Mark Peters, Wayne Mooney and Chuck Barnwell.

delivered it. I was ready for them as I had studied my information and presented it many times in the office. Then, the end came and it was time for questions. The only problem was that there were no questions from the audience. All that I can remember is thinking that it was career ending. It was the first time many of the chiefs had been introduced to me, face to face. What could have went wrong? Was I that bad? A couple of tormenting hours later I received an email from one of the command staff, saying how great the presentation was delivered. If the information is presented in a straightforward manner and all of the bases are covered there may not be questions and this is what was relayed to me. This is how I learned that sometimes no questions are good questions. And, after all it was not career ending.

Assertiveness vs. Aggressiveness

As Chief Eddie Buchanan and I discussed this particular portion, he thought that I should add a segment discussing the difference between an individual being aggressive and being assertive. Understanding the difference between the two could essentially, be the difference between being successful and unsuccessful as a leader. When you consider how a leader influences others, there are two approaches, one has a lasting impact while the other is typically short lived.

Aggressiveness is protecting your rights, beliefs and territory without any regard for other individuals. As there is no one correct answer to every problem, there is no one individual with all of the answers. Attempting to force individuals, without explaining, to believe as you do will not earn you any respect. While being aggressive on the fire ground can be an admirable trait of a strong individual, if it is uncoordinated or not part of the overall objective, freelancing can be deadly. The goal is to take the boldness of being aggressive and combine it with the respect for others and turn it into assertiveness.

As Chief Buchanan stated it, an assertive individual is one that protects their rights, beliefs and territory while respecting those of others. If an individual does not stand up for what they believe is right, they are basically showing traits of a distrusting behavior. The basis of what this country was established on exemplifies the assertiveness of our founding fathers. They did not believe that their rights and beliefs were being respected; in essence, the United States of America was born. I do believe that in the name of safety, training, and simply doing our job we need to take the same approach. Be the assertive individual that is consistent with their attitude and their need for knowing and performing the job well. Be the assertive individual that believes that training for the "ordinary" and "extraordinary" incidents will mentally and physically prepare us for whatever call we may run. As well, be the assertive individual that performs the job as a public servant because you believe in servant leadership. As a strong leader, you are serving the individuals that you stand before; they are watching your every move (remember behavior modeling from earlier).

Having a sense of pride and passion in our profession is paramount for an individual to be successful. What you choose to do with this pride and passion will be the determining factor of whether you succeed or fail. When you do decide to fight a battle, remember to side towards being more assertive than aggressive. While you want to show confidence and boldness with your beliefs, much more success will come with understanding and demonstrating respect for others opinions. In addition, being a leader is much more than just being passionate. If you are preparing to make a stand on a belief or right, know your materials by researching every aspect of it (Expert Power), even the ideas that oppose your opinion. Lastly, regardless of what, how, who or when – follow what your heart tells you and guides you to do (Referent Power); nothing that you do will matter if your heart is not in it. In the Fire Service, we need individuals that will make the commitment to being the individual that believes in safety, training, and accomplishing the job the way it is meant to be handled. Be that individual, if not for you, then for your family and the families of other firefighters. Be the Barn Boss.

Key Points

- Consider your Sources of Power and how they apply to different situations.

- Be engaged. Be smart and buy into the right things, do it because you believe in them.

- Firefighting isn't just a job; it's a way of life.

- Take care of your station, your department, and your community by being the best Damn Station in the Department.

- Remember your returns may come in the long run.

- It's ok to not be Mr. Popular, but make sure that you have the Courage to be Safe.

- Never back down from what you believe in, just be smart about the battles that you choose to fight.

- No questions can be good questions.

- Be Assertive – respect others but stand tall for what you believe in.

- Follow your heart.

Chapter 3

"Experience is at the cost of blood and grief"

Francis Brannigan

What are we doing?

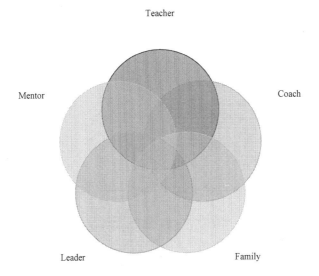

Teacher

Mentor

Coach

Leader

Family

The question that I want everyone to think about as we go through the rest of this book is, "What are we doing to take care of us?" "How does your station or department measure up when it comes to near misses, injuries and mistakes?" Looking at the big picture, what are we doing as a service? This is where the Barn Bosses have the greatest impact and influence. We have got a lot of things rolling right now, we are doing a lot of things right. We have the statistics, the figures, our mentality is changing to understand the science and its implications, and I think we are headed in the right direction. However, one of the things that I try to point out when I'm on the floor is that all accidents are "Predictable and Preventable." If we keep that in mind and always strive to predict and prevent incidents before they happen, we will accomplish our goal, we will be safer and better for it. I believe that if we educate ourselves and learn to practice the "foreseeability" word, we can continue to accomplish a lot and overcome major hurdles. In reality there are only a very few instances where a firefighter lost their life trying to save another. We sometimes forget about the Life- Big, Property- Small concept and trying to remember to not be complacent. This can be very difficult; especially at 2:00 am, running what we think should be a basic call that we run every day.

If you have not seen nor have any knowledge of the accident triangle and its line of progression, you should study it. There are different variations but essentially it suggest that 10,000 near misses equals 1 fatality. As we become accidentally successful and complacent overtime we will see numerous near misses and minor injuries – maybe even a few lost time accidents. After some amount of time if these situations are not confronted and stopped the department is bound to witness a catastrophic event.

My dad tells this story of me, which I do not recall, where I had a habit of confiscating his work tools – mainly screwdrivers. I would take his screwdrivers and I found it interesting to stick it in ant beds and watch the ants scramble. Apparently, this amused me and took up time as there is not much else a Pre-K Kid can do. Dad swears he warned me, however, this particular interest of mine kept me quiet and out of his hair so I really wonder how much he warned me.... On a regular basis I would waste time attacking ant beds with large screw drivers, obviously being accidently successful each time. However, on this one particular day a dirt mound had formed which appeared to me to resemble an ant bed. In addition, no one else identified this dirt mound as anything different than an ant bed either. Little did I know that when my manly screwdriver attacked the dirt mound, ants did not come out, a large swarm of yellow jackets tore my tail up. My parents, EMS will appreciate this – did not call the ambulance, they chose to drive me to the hospital with 30 plus yellow jacket stingers in me. They had no idea if I was allergic, but it wasn't a real emergency they said..... Lesson of the story is to determine what your ant beds are and correct it before it becomes a yellow jacket nest and tears your tail up.

During one live fire training program for certified firefighters we invited companies from the field to come up and assist the academy in delivery of the training. The participants met our qualifications and had received live fire adjunct training prior to this particular day. We typically would allow the in-service crews to serve as the crew leaders and academy staff served as the safety's and incident commanders. This particular day I was serving as the interior safety officer for a one room burn with the objectives of performing a primary search and fire extinguishment. The crew consisted of two highly capable and qualified individuals with a company officer watching over them. My duty was to stand in the background and observe, the only interaction I should have is if I foresaw any safety related issues starting to occur.

The team suited up and made entry into a smoke filled structure with a 1 ¾" hoseline. The report was a structure fire with unknown entrapments. I quickly followed in behind the team with a thermal imaging camera and watched as they quickly checked behind the front

GCFES Burn Building where we conducted 200+ burns just for recruit schools per year.

door for victims, swiped out as far as they could reach to the center of the room and continued their search down the hallway. The nozzle man made it to the room of origin and quickly extinguished the fire. At this point, they had not found any victims, however they still had half the structure to search. They constructed their plan and continued on a right hand search into the next room and located an adult victim. They quickly packaged the patient in the smoke filled environment with limited visibility and made their way to the exterior of the structure. The victim was passed to outside crews and the search team gathered up and re-entered the structure to complete their primary search. As they were driving down the hallway to their last known location I noticed the Team Lead suddenly stopped, head dropped down, and then his arms buckled – face planting into the floor. This entire series of events occurred in five seconds and the moment that I noticed this, his search partner did as well. I moved in to assist in the extrication as his teammate oriented him for a quick extrication towards the nearest exit. We each grabbed a shoulder strap and extricated him within 30 seconds. Luckily, he had a vasovagal response and nothing more serious – however, none-the-less it scared all of us.

Some items I learned from this series of events include:

1) You never know when something could occur.

2) Although we had trained for the mayday response, it did not work textbook as I forgot to call a mayday. The moment I saw the event play out, I reacted to the firefighters needs. If the extrication would have been prolonged it may have turned out different, however, when we exited the structure no one knew what had just occurred.

3) There was a company officer assigned to watch over the team, however, this officer had lost track of the team and failed to call a mayday or assist in the extrication. Plan for this, train for this – the down firefighter's partner was on top of the entire situation. Don't take for granted that we will rise to the situation.

4) Take near misses such as this and apply them to other training situations. There was nothing about this event

which could not have occurred in any structure fire, in any town in America.

If you have the chance to sit in on a "Courage to be Safe" class, do it. I have never sat through a class where I learned more about my own fire service attitude and awareness for what goes on in the service. Chief Billy Hayes did an outstanding job in Hall County that day. We have to change our mentality to have that courage to say enough is enough. During my time as a Gwinnett County Training Officer I was able to implement this class in the Acting Officer Course on day one in order to set the tone for the remaining 120 hours of training.

Where can the Barn Boss go to get information?

There are tons of materials and information that are out there just for us and a vast majority of it is free. We just need to know where to find information. One of the articles that I authored for FireEngineering.com, "LODD: What can you do to prevent them?," had a large amount of internet based materials that were broken down by categories such as scenarios, building construction, instructor, fire clowns, and fire service history to name a few. There are about 30 different categories of internet based sites that are free or very low cost that I have used in some capacity at the station level. The information is out there, we just need to know where to go to get it. A comprehensive list of these categories is posted on www.FireServiceSLT.com under resources, more on this site later.

The Barn Boss needs this type of exposure, they need to understand what is out there and how to use it. The other nugget of knowledge I would throw out there is to go to a conference whether it is FDIC or the Metro Atlanta Firefighters Conference. It is your responsibility to expand your horizons and look outside your bay walls.

TRADE

If you are not a part of NFA's TRADE (Training Resources and Data Exchange) program, you need to be (http://www.usfa.fema.gov/training/nfa/programs/trade.html). TRADE was created in 1984 in order to address the difficulties that state and local fire training systems were experiencing in relation to spreading educational materials. You can send an email with your question or need and they will put it on their bi-weekly newsletter that is free and send it to 20,000 people across the country. The other part of this program is the information that the Louisiana State University keeps on their database has every program that you could ever dream of for training or policies, anything you can think of.

TRADE Objectives:
- Identify fire, rescue and emergency medical services training needs at the regional level.
- Identify and exchange training programs and resources within regions and, whenever possible, replicate those resources.

- Identify national trends with an impact on fire-related training and education.
- Provide to the National Fire Academy an annual assessment of fire training resource needs within the region, together with recommendations as to how TRADE can better support federal, state and local fire training systems.

International Society of Fire Service Instructors (ISFSI)

This organization has a plethora of resources available to any member. This is an organization where you truly get out of it, what you put into it. A large majority of my experiences have come from being a part of this organization. They commonly ask for volunteers and I commonly throw my name in. Due to this organization I have the privilege of traveling the country teaching various topics. I have sat in the AFG grant reviews and sat on the grant criteria development team, all because they asked for a volunteer. They now have created the Program Share which goes out in their weekly newsletter. The intent of the program is for any individual needing assistance with a topic or question to contact the office and they will post your topic/question on the front page of the newsletter going to thousands of people. The last individual that provided a question responded that he was overwhelmed with instant information. The ISFSI also has a Members Only Section where information is dropped into a database by members and all you do is type in what topic you are looking for and there it is. Instant information for any topic.

Mentoring

Why is mentoring so important? What value can be gained from such a program, formally or informally? Mentoring in practice is the fostering of a relationship between an experienced veteran who shares his knowledge and experience with a less experienced firefighter or officer. Although this may sound simple enough in theory, we sometimes don't allow ourselves to gain all of the benefits that can come from a mentorship.

"It's the chance to pass on knowledge and experience that cannot be found in a book or a PowerPoint® program."

The word mentor comes from Greek mythology. Mentor (Greek God) was the counselor to Odysseus and wise tutor of his son Telemachus. Mentor came to be described as a wise and experienced individual. Mentoring in practice is the fostering of a relationship between an experienced veteran who shares his or her knowledge and experience with a less experienced firefighter or officer; or just a different capability. Build yourself a network, have people in your department and surrounding areas that you can go to for help; you can always count on them. On a whole, the Fire Service is more than willing to share information, and help you with whatever you need. If you're anything like me I know that I am not the smartest one of there, I have no option but to surround myself with people smarter than me.

I have had the privilege of working with and for some great crews and officers throughout my career. I can count them all the way from being a volunteer through to my career department. I had to show that I was committed to what I was a part of and then they took the interest in making sure that I reached whatever potential I could. They wanted to help me climb that mountain, I just had to put the gear on and start climbing. However, I have never been a part of any formal mentoring program. They have all been people that have looked to bring me up or I sought them out and would not leave until I got all of the information I could out of them. In Retired Phoenix, Arizona Fire Chief Alan Brunacini's No Brainer Management Series, he provides information from one of his mentors on what he calls a real simple set of basic boss behaviors – these boss behaviors include:

> *1) Tell your people what to do (expectations, but not micromanaging),*
> *2) Give your people the training and tools to do the job (share knowledge and skills),*
> *3) Get out of your peoples way (allow the firefighters to charge forward), and*
> *4) Tell your firefighter how they did when they finish (provide constructive feedback).*

As many of my mentors have come from inside my current department and from the stations where I worked; just as many have come from outside my department and from different states all together.

I had the honor of being one of Georgia's Advocates for the Everyone Goes Home (EGH) Program, but I did not get there on my own. It was with the help of (National Advocate Manager at that time) Columbia Southern University Vice President of Admissions, Marketing and Outreach Billy Hayes and Columbia Southern University Director of Training and Professional Development (Region VIII Advocate at the time) Ron Dennis. Chief Dennis came to Georgia to teach a Battalion Chief Development Class with Billy and they started talking about EGH and I started asking questions from that point on. To his credit, his response was always, "Hey, if you are asking questions that just means you're thinking and doing." Over the course of the next couple of months, the Georgia Advocate spot became available and of all the people that could have been asked they selected a 23-year-old firefighter. They apparently saw something in me that made them think that I would do a good job. I am still looking for what they saw but since that point, and after traveling around the state teaching our program I would like to think that I have made a difference.

This was just one example and there are so many more. The basis of the example is people are there to help you; you just have to put yourself out there and create your own mentoring program. I did not know that was what I was doing until years later when I looked back and said, "Hey, these people have really made a difference in my life and career." It is great to know that I can pick up the phone, call any one of these people, and have an answer today.

In the Fire Engineering article *Mentoring: Perspectives of the Rookie and Veteran*, David Rhodes and I discuss the two sides of mentoring. On the new firefighter side, you have to be willing to listen, take constructive criticism and be committed to hard work. Frank Viscuso provides the required attributes of a prospective mentee as – Eager to Grow/Change, Willingness to Invest Time, Positive Attitude, Respectful, Purposeful, Confident, Loyal and Willing to be Accountable. One of the prime examples, concerning listening, I encountered early in my career concerned the building construction features of a church built in the early 1900s in my former first-in district. This church had been renovated and changed hands several times. While conducting a preplan, we learned from one of the veterans who grew up in the area and watched the church evolve over the years that the church had three rain roofs built one on top of the other. How important is it to have this information? Without his experience, we would never have known.

On the veteran side, you have to use explicit mentoring and create opportunities for mentoring. Find ways to make yourself available. One of the most important roles veteran members have is to pass along the street knowledge that only experience brings. This experience includes lessons learned at the task, tactical, and strategic levels. There are always opportunities to pass along knowledge to new firefighters who show interest and remind you of yourself. You know the type–the "sponge" that asks a million questions and is actively engaged. As a veteran, these individuals keep you going because they are so motivated and uncorrupted by the years of misaligned expectations between the administration and line officers. These members make up the 10 percenters who get things done. What do we do about the other 90 percent? As a veteran member, you have to let go of wanting to be the star of the show and focus your attention on creating stars.

Some suggestions for ways to create opportunities include the following:

- Approve training requests (say yes more than you say no).
- Suggest training courses.
- Involve members in department projects.
- Match talent to organizational needs
- Talk about the members' weaknesses, and suggest ways of overcoming them.
- Invite members to attend meetings with you.

Picking a Mentor

Look around your station or department and find the individuals who seem to always know what is going on, those who put their hands on the tools even though it's not truck day. On incident scenes, they operate without orders (not freelancing); they always seem to know what has to be done, why it needs to be done, and when to do it, and they always maintain their composure no matter what is going on. They are reliable and consistent.

Look for the individuals who always have a positive attitude about work and the desire to be a little bit better every day. Positive attitudes are contagious and will help you stay focused on the organization's mission and forget about what "I" want. These same individuals are those who constantly ask questions and try to figure out more efficient methods to perform the job and a proactive approach to problem solving. They consider it their personal responsibility to send everyone home in the same condition they came to work that very day. On top of that, they make it their responsibility to send the same people into retirement the same way they entered the job, as healthy as can be.

Creating the Mentorship

After finding that role model that you want to mold yourself after, jump in their back pocket and soak up every bit of information you can. As the less experienced individual in the mentorship, you have to be devoted to training, take the initiative to get out there, and put your hands on the tools when no one else is. You also have to be willing to take advice and constructive criticism to build the relationship to where everyone involved is comfortable exchanging knowledge and experience. More often than not, the less experienced individuals have to prove themselves in the station. As this occurs and these individuals become successful in their daily operations, the experienced firefighters take notice. They start to ask themselves what they can do to impart their knowledge and experience to the people who need it and will value it.

As all of this happens, after a little hard work, you begin to build a mentorship with the more experienced personnel. Hopefully, this mentorship will increase your knowledge, help with your situational awareness, and advance your career beyond anything that you would have accomplished by yourself. That last point is very important to remember. No matter how hard I have worked or what I have accomplished, everything that I have been involved with has been directly related to someone giving me a chance, someone believing that I could "lead up." All things are possible if you open your ears and embrace all the opportunities around you. A closing example for this type of mentorship occurred when I got involved in Everyone Goes Home (EGH) as the Georgia Advocate. National Advocate Manager Billy Hayes and Assistant Chief (Retired) Ron Dennis, Avondale, AZ., saw my devotion to firefighter safety. They chose to mentor me in the EGH program; I became the Georgia Advocate in a very short time period. Ultimately, I was named one of the Top 20 Instructors in the country and received the Seal of Excellence for Leadership and Safety at the National Fire Academy

from the National Fallen Firefighters Foundation roughly two years later. Through personal examples, I have laid out two results on opposite

realms of mentoring, but they are both direct benefits of mentoring and the success that can come with it on the fire ground and in your career. (Picture R to L – Billy, myself and Ron Dennis at the National Fire Academy accepting the Seal of Excellence)

Creating Opportunities

David Rhodes provides this excerpt concerning creating opportunities: "One of the most overlooked mentoring techniques is the creation of opportunities for your members. Your members also need to get outside your organization and learn how other organizations do things. This exposure creates a well-rounded individual who will appreciate the things your organization is doing right and bring back suggestions on how to improve things that may be getting done better elsewhere. You also need to pull individuals out of their comfort zone. If we don't do this, we end up with great fire ground commanders who can't compose a memo or an administrative genius who writes a manual on how to write memos but can't command a vehicle fire. Look for opportunities for your members to become involved in projects or training that they probably would not volunteer for on their own."

"Some individuals are afraid of formal mentoring programs because they don't think that everyone should be a mentor. We have to face the fact that everyone is a mentor whether we want them to be or not. I have learned many lessons from those styles and personalities that I did not

particularly like or identify with. These individuals taught me a lot about what not to do if given the opportunity to handle a similar situation. These lessons are just as important, if not more important, than learning from the best member in the organization, because they are based on real life. We can't shelter our members from bad leaders and bad decision makers, but we should formally force them to spend time with those who exhibit competence and live by our organizational values. This balance (Yen and Yang) is good for the members' development and helps them develop their own style."

Who's Idea is it?

The saying, "I don't have one original idea that I came up with on my own; everything that I have accomplished is owed to somebody else." I may be stretching by saying I don't have any original ideas, however, the point is that mentors helped me achieve that original idea. I try and take what is around me and without reinventing the wheel make it better, but I never came up with any grand idea that solved all the problems in the world. However, this is one of the great things about the Fire Service though; we can jump on each other's ideas, and develop some quality materials. Firefighters are really of a different breed, we're very creative in whatever we do and our determination is immeasurable. If you tell a firefighter to take out a masonry wall with a ball ping hammer, you give them enough time they will have a hole big enough to drive a custom cab through.

Being involved in the private industry for many years now, there was one situation where I was invited to a fire service event as an advisor and was unrelated to any products my private employer sold or purchased. I asked for support from my employer and their response (based on their current knowledge) was I needed to take vacation because it would be a conflict of interest. When I told them that I was offering my services for free, they could not believe it – it is not something that is considered in the private sector, you always get compensated. We, as firefighters, should really be grateful for what we have in the fire service that is not offered in the private sector. Now, that does not mean everything should be free, you have to select what you do. However, if you have never been outside of the public service you may not know how great it is.

Make it Personal

I do not know how many of you have signed the Seat Belt Pledge from the Everyone Goes Home Program. I am sure that most of our departments have policies about wearing your seat belt and are taught to wear it from the first day of Recruit School. Even if you have policies in place, and it is required to be worn by everyone, you should still take the Pledge or make your own commitment to wear it. I will tell you what it did for me. I have been the worlds worse about not wearing my seat belt, yet I knew it was policy and it could save my life if something happened. That was not enough for some reason, and I still do not know why it was not enough. Here is where it got me though, I signed up for something bigger than just me, just one person, when I signed the Pledge. I sent the Pledge to every member of my department accompanied by a letter that I wrote. I did not tell them they better wear it, or make any threats; I do not think that I even told them that it was our policy. I talked about the families without their whole family, the national accident rate, and about pulling out one of my friends from their vehicle as a volunteer.

I was a volunteer for about four years and I was out to eat with a family friend (Milton's) when we were coming back from a neighboring town restaurant and we got the call. We received numerous motor vehicle accident calls at this particular intersection over the years so there was nothing abnormal about the situation. However, I had never responded to or thought about what it would be like to respond to a friend involved in an accident. Upon arrival all I remember is that I knew that truck, but it could not be, right? It could not be the truck that I rode in previously. I arrived first on scene along with my friend Kevin who was a firefighter/EMT. We quickly assessed the situation and broke up into teams with a few of the other responders. Working on the passenger side of the vehicle, there was no entrapment but obvious spider webbing of the windshield, likely from the impact of my friend's skull. I wound up pulling a high school friend and a buddy from his truck where it did not appear that neither he nor his passenger wore their seatbelts. All I remember now is him fighting us, being combative, and then arriving at the hospital a few hours later to see the outcome. They suffered the usual items – concussion, swelling of the brain and had to relearn some things but they fortunately recovered. Seeing this should scare you or at least focus you on educating those that you know – those are the ones that you can affect individually. The other side of the story is that you will never know what you will find or what call you will run, which can be difficult.

I spoke of values and beliefs and what that seat belt means; I talked about wearing it for your families, if nothing else. When I wrote the letter I described earlier I knew from that point it was enough for me to go home to my family, it was enough for me to not be a statistic, it was enough for me to not cause a funeral for my brothers and sisters. It took me a long time to change my way of thinking, but not everyone is that lucky.

Results of the Georgia Seat Belt Blitz

Not only did I make a plea to my department I obtained the mailing address of every fire chief in the State of Georgia and with the help of a dear friend and colleague, Leslie Kalmbach, we wrote a personal letter and mailed it to every one of them. 640 departments – from volunteer to metro size. In all, 2,780 firefighters signed the pledge to wear their seat belts during this blitz. I have to say that this was also an effort that would not have been possible without the help of Billy Hayes securing the funding for materials and postage.

Honor Those Before Us!!!

I was recently invited and attended the Tampa 2 Summit as a delegate for the ISFSI. The event was put together by the National Fallen Firefighters Foundation (NFFF) in February 2014 where we discussed honoring those before us. We revisited the initiatives set forth in Tampa ten years prior in 2004. We set out to see what was working and what needed to change. The goal of reducing LODDs by 25% in 5 years and 50% in 10 years was set in 2004 and unfortunately we did not make it. So, how do you affect change? Fredrick Von Mises' book, Human Action, describes how humans must feel uncomfortable before we are willing to make a change. I was uncomfortable when I arrived on the scene of my buddy's truck with friends inside. So, how do we make firefighters feel uncomfortable? We have to honor those that lost their lives and learn from the situations where everything went wrong even in the best of circumstances. We have to put ourselves in the same situations and think through the what would "I" do in this exact situation. I have to make myself feel uncomfortable by understanding my limitations and working to improve my shortcomings.

Maybe, just maybe, someday our Line of Duty Deaths will reflect those of outside the U.S. We have to keep plugging away at the LODD numbers, get the word out and expose Firefighter's and EMS personnel to new ideas, new technology, new research and awareness of what is going on around us. This is what the National Fallen Firefighters Foundation is attempting to accomplish, along with many other organizations, trying to make this a safer business by honoring those before us. "The only unforgivable mistake is the one that you make again." Anonymous Marines.

I discuss in the Training Officer's Boot Camp the Francis Brannigan quote "Experience is at the cost of blood and grief." We may have never been involved in a LODD or a catastrophic event, however, somebody somewhere experienced these hardships and passed on the information so that we could learn from these situations. We have the obligation to learn from them and pass on the knowledge and skills so that the blood and grief is not quite so much. Someone paid the ultimate sacrifice for us to know what we know today, honor them by studying your craft.

Sharing the Knowledge

Another idea that I cannot take credit for but I have become involved in, is creating a training association for surrounding departments. The Metro Atlanta Fire Chiefs Association created a sub-section called Metro Atlanta Training Officers (MATO) Association. I was selected to be the Vice-Chairman in 2009 and then selected as the Chairman of the Association in 2010. The Chiefs govern MATO but they essentially run as an independent Association. There are around 36 departments from the area that are involved and this allows us to talk about, create, and distribute training freely amongst each other. What is even better is that my department then, Gwinnett County Fire and Emergency Services (GCFES), backed my participation 100%, as they were interested in what was next. They asked what else was possible? GCFES had not been involved in the surrounding departments for many years, kind of operating as their own state to some degree, however their mentality had changed. Even to this day seven years later, they are still heavily involved in MATO. They want to be involved in the service, not just what is going on in Gwinnett.

All of this was said, to simply say, do something. There is so much out there that we are doing right. So, get involved, every single individual in the service has the opportunity and influence to make a difference. Lead by example, do not be afraid of those people in the cheap seats, they will come around once they see you are true at heart with what you are trying to

"Get involved, every single individual in the service has the opportunity and influence to Make A Difference."

accomplish. And, if that still doesn't work for a select few – beat them with the influencers that are on board.

FireServiceSLT

I mentioned that I would talk about it later so here it is, FireServiceSLT: Safety, Leadership and Training. This was a website that I created in order to promote the Gwinnett County

Leadership and Safety Conference in 2009 – 2010 and nothing more. I created it on the premises that three things will take care of firefighters: Safety, Leadership, and Training. It was my belief even then that we needed to conduct meaningful training, study and educate ourselves, and we needed good leaders to guide us. However, over the years it evolved into much more as it became a place where I started to share training materials – videos, PowerPoints, and PDFs. Any individual can go to the website and scroll through the list of training materials under the training tab and download it for free (there are two pages worth of informational links to stored materials). There is also a full web page of resource links to other websites which offer training at little to no cost, or they are educational in nature. As well, I post updates on new "fire service stuff."

Eventually, this concept evolved into the SLT Mental Model which describes how leadership qualities of an individual is cultured through the three main topics – Safety, Leadership and Training.

Since 2010, the Metro Atlanta Firefighters Conferences has developed themselves as the go to conference in Georgia with all the resources and have done an amazing job. I have been honored to instruct here since its inception and can tell you it is a premier conference. As a firefighter in the south you have to attend this conference (Metro Atlanta Firefighters Conference – MAFFC.org) their classrooms are free and the practical's are minimum cost for materials).

These Barn Bosses Get It! And, thank you for allowing me to be along for the ride!

SLT Mental Model

As described above, the SLT Mental Model depicts how a leader is formed. The various sub-topics such as building muscle memory, no fail training, domains of learning, decision making capabilities, leadership styles, mentoring applications and generational differences are explored to understand their differences as well as how they connect with one another.

Safety and Training are connected together to form the foundation of the mental model with sub-topics such as muscle memory and decision making capabilities creating the bonds. Safety and Training provide the pathways which lead to a leadership role, formal or informal. Within these pathways, Leadership is learned and developed through experiences (training, life, education, or work experiences). At the top of the pyramid is the capstone, Leadership, which eventually holds all of the attributes/experiences developed over time – and makes you an authentic leader.

By design, when this workshop is given there are no PowerPoint distractions or the crutch of reading slides. The attendee's attention is to be captured through the lost art of communicating with peers and depicting situations, experiences and solutions with personable techniques. This is an open dialogue with audience interaction. This approach helps the audience understand the power of this mental model and its deliverables. As you are reading this play over in your mind the conversation you would encounter if you were sitting in this presentation. I challenge you to think back to the very beginning of this book and include any item you may have learned or idea sparked and include it in this conversation.

As mentioned earlier, the SLT Mental Model really came much later in my career, it was only after serving in multiple leadership capacities in the public safety and private sector. Regardless of the position held, there were several key items which have proven to withstand the differences of environments but also serve as a foundation for developing the people around you, including myself. This mental model is designed to provide an avenue to develop your own authentic style of leadership without being trapped inside the textbook paradigm of what leaders are supposed to look like.

Although the mental model its self is only discussed briefly here, everything inside of this text is built into the mental model.

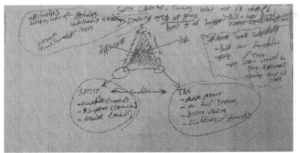 *Picture – First hand written example of the mental model, and yes I failed penmanship.*

How it all comes together

If we train the right way and we are good at what we do, we will be safe. Safety is not just something we do or you pass a test and now you are "Safe." Safety comes from being technically competent, physically sound, and having situational awareness. If we are safe, we will be constantly training and developing our technical competencies so that we can make good decisions. Our physical abilities will be exercised and our limitations understood. The knowledge gained through experiences and structured training such as Tactical Decision Games (identified earlier) will enhance our ability to identify, understand and predict the emergency – situational awareness.

If we have good leadership, you got it, we will be safe and we will be training. This is the whole concept of FireServiceSLT: Safety. Leadership and Training. It eventually comes full circle. When I started thinking about the creation of this site it was originally just for a conference that I was starting in the Atlanta area. As time went on though, I started thinking there is more that I can do with this. There will hopefully be many people looking at the site so why not post all of the training and resources that I have for everyone to use. So, now there is about 40 different structured PowerPoint programs (most I did not create) and 30 or so website resource links that I have used and broke down into categories for people to choose from quickly what they are looking for. It's all about sharing.

Key Points

- Look at what you, your department, and the national fire service as a whole are doing.

- Life is BIG, Property conservation is small when it comes to risk vs. benefit.

- Think about using foreseeability to prevent accidents. Most, if not all are preventable.

- Use your resources.

- Create your own informal mentoring program. Surround yourself with the people that care about the service and what happens to our brothers and sisters. These people will be your greatest allies throughout your career.

- Make it personal and Honor Those Before Us!

- If you think there is something that could be better, then take the initiative to make it better.

Chapter 4

"Leadership and learning are indispensable to each other."

John Fitzgerald Kennedy

Stepping Up and Stepping Out

Stepping Up and Stepping Out means, simply, doing what is right – to not be afraid of those around us. The methods we elect to use for achieving what is right can be different for some of us, but as long as our values and beliefs are in the right place we can't go wrong. We may trip, we may even fall flat on our face but we will get back up. *"Luck is the crossroads of hard work and opportunity."* Sometimes what is right will not win you votes but it will earn you respect, which will never be forgotten. The other aspect to Stepping Up and Stepping Out is focused on doing what others will not or in some cases others just haven't created the opportunity for themselves. It may be taking the hard road and accepting the risk of working on a special assignment for the department, or setting up your career so that you are given these special opportunities. I do not believe in the typical sense of luck, luck is the crossroads of hard work and opportunity.

This entire book builds upon itself, and weaves each chapter in and out of each other. That is due to the fact that if you represent one of these chapters then most of you will represent *all* of these chapters. So far, we have talked about leading as the Barn Boss, Knowing our job and Doing our job, Being Engaged, and Honoring Those Before Us. We've got all of the resources and information, we are engaged and we know our job. So, what do we do now? We Step Up and Step Out!!

Just Believe

In order to have the chance to Step Up and Step Out we have to recognize what is important to us. Do we value what Chief Rick Lasky talks about, "Pride, Integrity, and Honesty?" We should! Gwinnett County Fire and Emergency Services (GCFES) believes in values so much that Retired Fire Chief Bill Myers made it a point to attend every Recruit School class to explain the meaning behind Truth, Trust, Respect, and Unity. These are referred to as their Core Values. The U.S. Army refers to theirs as Values and Attributes, there are seven values and sixteen attributes which an officer is evaluated against. This is what they stand for and how they govern themselves. I guess you could say that this is the "Law of the Land" in a sort of way.

U.S. Army Values	U.S. Army Attributes
1. Honor	1. Mental
	2. Physical
2. Integrity	3. Emotional
	4. Conceptual
3. Courage	5. Interpersonal
	6. Technical
4. Loyalty	7. Tactical
	8. Communicating
5. Respect	9. Decision-Making
	10. Motivating
6. Selfless-Service	11. Planning
	12. Executing
7. Duty	13. Assessing
	14. Developing
	15. Building
	16. Learning.

Here's a brief look at what each of the Gwinnett County Fire and Emergency Services Core Values stand for:

Truth

We have to be truthful to ourselves. We know what is right, that gut instinct is usually right, we should follow it more. We have to be truthful to our fellow firefighters, this is our family. There is nothing more morally degrading than firefighters bickering at one another or fighting over what is nothing more than something that is usually trivial to begin with. Last but not least we have to be truthful to our customers. Our customers, our citizens, feel safe when they are around us. Do not tell them something when it is not so, be honest and open. Some of us will learn the hard way before it sticks.

Trust

Right along with Truth is Trust. When we enter a burning building we have to trust that our backup is right there with us and vice versa. Retired FDNY Battalion Chief John Salka's "First In, Last Out: Leadership Lessons of FDNY" literature is based on this principle. It says exactly so on the back cover, "Would the people that work for you follow you into a burning building?" In the Fire Service, there is no room for someone that you cannot trust; there is too much riding on the line every time we get on the rig.

During one point as a recruit school instructor I ran into this exact incident. One of the recruits was struggling with a drill so a group that had already completed the drill packed out and finished the drill with this individual, actually most of the class. However, there was one individual that expressed out loud that they wouldn't do the drill again for their best friend. Later that day, one of the other recruits in this individuals group, who had never seen fire before, told the instructors that he was a little nervous going into the Firefighter I burns. His concern was "What if something happens and I need their help?" He had a valid point, the trust had been lost. However, we cannot just terminate them because of what they said. Everything eventually worked out, turned out the "problem" did not want to be a part of the fire service anyway and removed their selves.

Our citizens trust that we will take care of them and provide the best care imaginable. They trust that we will take care of their every belonging. They trust us because of the badge we wear- which we will explain later what exactly it means to wear it on your chest – do not give them a reason to not trust us. Do not be our own worst enemy. In 2010, GCFES had been the recipient of 17 straight years of SPLOST (Special Purpose Local Option Sales Tax), which was approved by the citizens. This does not happen without community trust and this funding furnishes stations, trucks and other equipment which is not counted in the year to year operating budget.

Respect

Respect, it can be hard to define but you definitely know it when you see it. This is the acknowledgement that most of the people in this world have some value. I will not say all, but most.

They may not be like you or even agree with your way of accomplishing tasks, but they have a value. Make sure that you respect your fellow firefighters, your veterans, your company officers, our citizens, and most importantly yourself by treating them how you want to be treated. When you do not show respect for yourself, it is seldom shown to others. Respect can be as simple as yes sir and yes ma'am. Be Positive, be upbeat, and be motivated. Respect the diversity that each individual brings to the kitchen table (skills, backgrounds, life experience, etc.)

Unity

What is the old saying? "There is no "I" in team." Unity is vital for what we do on a daily basis, day-to-day operations. There is no one person which will ever conquer a fire ground and if they think that they can, they are probably going to injure someone or

their self. The fire service is a Brotherhood; we unite around one another when one of us is in a time of need. We are there for each other when one of us is down, we check on each other. It does not matter if you are a firefighter in Grande Prairie, Canada or Thomasville, Georgia; you are still a firefighter and you will be recognized as so. They will open their home and station to you, all because you wear a patch. Every time I see a LODD I cringe, even though I have never met them. Nevertheless, I feel for them and their families, because that was a member of the Brotherhood, that was part of my family and I know that could have just as easily been me.

One of the greatest examples of unity that I witnessed early on happened one night when a gunshot incident was dispatched at Station 14. Unbeknownst to most, it was the address of a department captain. Upon arrival responders found the captain's son accidentally wounded from a gunshot, with blood stained walls. This captain was out of town during this event but as expected quickly returned to be there for his son, who was in the ICU and survived the accident. The firefighters at Station 14 came together, fixed and cleaned the entire house before the captain got home. They spent their own money and time to make this happen, and it was a big deal that meant a lot to this family. This family never had to deal with or see the mess that was created as they tended to their son, who they were unsure would survive for quite some time.

Another situation that our family faced involves a brother firefighter that discovered he had cancer and he could not work due to all of the treatments. Our fire family came together and worked his shifts for him as swap time so that he can continue to collect a paycheck and keep his insurance while he is getting treatments. At one point, there was about five months of shifts worked for him, all from people devoting their time just to help his family. That is unity!

That is the true meaning of brotherhood (Unity) and what it stands for! You do not find that in any other industry but in the fire service.

The same word choices may not be used by you or your organization but they are probably fairly close if you have them. For example, the values of FireServiceSLT are Integrity, Value Creation, Customer Focus, Teamwork and Fulfillment. It does not matter if we use one to replace another as long as they have meaning and that everyone inside the organization is working towards the common values. If we can do that, there is nothing we cannot accomplish.

Integrity – Doing what is right, even when no one is watching.

Value Creation – Strive for opportunities to create value in all realms, personally and professionally.

Customer Focus – Servant Leadership, anticipate the needs of your employees and those you are mentoring.

Teamwork – Always work as a team. There is no "I" in any fire service task. Look for the strengths in others and empower those around you.

Fulfillment – Find fulfillment in what you do. Provide a sense of pride in your work and understand the meaning of knowledge sharing.

Applying these values locally and at the station are so much more than just the words and definitions but to practice them where all crew members can see them are immeasurable to the success of your crew. During the Georgia Smoke Diver program I was teamed up with another candidate from the City of Marietta Fire Department. We had never encountered each other in the service and knew nothing of each other's values. As we met the first day we discussed how we prepared for the class and some of our backgrounds. We were quietly sizing each other up. In the GSD program, every task is completed with a partner and your partner can make or break you. As we went through the week several of the other teams were broke up due to candidates dropping out of the program. Some were required to even change two or three times during this training. For these individuals, the ones that graduated, they truly earned it. However, Will Daniels and I stayed team members throughout the entire program. We certainly benefited from gaining knowledge of each other's weaknesses and strengths each day. As the days were marked off, our bodies grew tired and sore, but our desire to finish the drill became stronger.

Even though I had physically and mentally prepared to the best of my ability there were still many trials and tribulations, and doubt – lots of doubt. We learned to complete one drill at a time and stay focused on just that one specific task. However, other

"In life, learn to complete one drill at a time and stay focused on that one specific task."

obstacles would attempt to deter me from my goal. Your turnout gear stays wet from the sweat we had this particular week and the freezing rain was an everyday obstacle to overcome. Due to these issues and not having appropriate clothing I began to suffer from severe chaffing and once it began it felt that it became worse by the hour. At the end of the day I would do everything possible in order to help the healing, however it was never enough. On day 4 during one of our drills, I had lost my pliers, which you are required to never lose. These pliers represent your ability to extricate your self during an entrapment, they represent attention to detail and I had lost mine. The instructors had located my pliers however they were unsure whose they were and held them to the end of the day.

The previous night my wounds had become intolerable and I was completely unsure how I was going to finish the program. It was to the point that during the drills I would actual open up the wounds and bleed. I made the decision that third night that I was going to finish the program, I had come too far to quit now. So, I placed sterile gauze on the wounds and wrapped my thighs with duct tape for the remaining days of the program. It was a painful choice but the only choice other than tapping out. My partner, Will, knew of the situation and the choice I had made.

As the end of the day drew to a close, it was time to pay the bank for losing my pliers. Paying the bank meant additional physical training (PT) after the 12 hour day of drills. At this point, you are sleep deprived, total body soreness, depleted of nutrients and still have one or two hours of work to do at night prepping gear for the next day. As the instructors asked for who did not have their pliers I went to raise my hand and Will stopped me. Will raised his hand and took the PT for me. We never told anyone or even discussed it after it was complete. He didn't think twice about his choice. We went on to complete the program as the only team that was not required to change members. In Will's one action, he represented everything we have discussed. I would not have held it against him or even asked him to pay the bank but he did it for something more than himself – the team.

Do What's Right

We have discussed values and their importance within an organization. So, how do we use these to Step Up and Step Out, gain the respect from the people around us. I mentioned that this process or mentality will not always win you many votes, make you rich, or get you the five bugels, but you will be able to sleep at night. You will be able to sleep knowing you did what was right.

This was depicted through an article in the September 2007 edition of Fire Engineering Magazine discussing a call from Clarke County, Nevada. The acting driver on the first-in engine stepped up when he saw a wall starting to lean on a tilt slab commercial structure. No one else seemed to notice, as crews were pre-occupied with operational task, including crews working on two sides of the burning structure. When he notified the IC on scene, the IC immediately called for an evacuation and started a Personnel Accountability Report (PAR). As they were evacuating, a collapse occurred, a PAR was started and a second collapse occurred. Remember that a tilt slab wall is dependent on the roof, when it goes everything is going to go. The IC conducted a second PAR and all personnel were accounted for with no injuries. This was all because of an acting driver stepping up to say what he saw. He saved two different crews from at least minimum injuries and at worst multiple LODDs.

Think Outside-of-I 285

Within the area I work, Metropolitan Atlanta, Interstate 285 makes an entire loop through the surrounding counties and around the City of Atlanta. A while back I was in a class with many of the other area departments and one of the individuals in the class was explaining how they try to get people to Step Up and Step Out, or "think-outside-the-box," or "think-outside-of-Interstate 285." This was their customized analogy for this very same concept. Most of you are asking how does "thinking-outside-of-Interstate 285" and Core Values come together. Well, it matters very much what your Core Values are, people want to know where you are coming from, where is your heart. Is your heart in the right place? What are your motives for looking outside the box or I 285? Are you Stepping Up for the right reasons or is there strictly a personal agenda.

Stepping Up matters, I am not so naïve to think that everything that is done is because it's always "just good for the company," but is the heart in the right place in everything that you are doing? Think of it as a "Gut Check Analysis;" examine the reasons why, your current position, and where you will we be at the end, what is the benefit and who will gain from it?

If the benefit is all for personal gain then it may not always a good idea and you will may lose credibility depending on the situation. On the flip side, if it has anything to do with saving lives, just one life, it's a good idea. Now in saying that, most fire departments are very strapped for cash, especially the last few years, so it may be a good idea but ask is it practical? In Chief John Salka's book "First In, Last Out," he actually states this concept perfectly. The segment is called Bootstrapping. "It simply means doing it as cheaply and efficiently as possible." Now saving that one life is good, but is there another project or idea that can save a larger majority of lives, this is a great idea. With most fire departments current position, this is not only encouraged, it's the only option, if we want to achieve anything at all. So, go bootstrapping. Remember, a Barn Boss influence and leadership do not cost money.

Take the Risk

The risk is great but the possible benefits from turning out a product greater than the command staff imagined can pay huge dividends in the end. They will remember the person who stepped up to the plate when the department needed them, who was willing to go the extra mile even when it wasn't required. My hat is off to GCFES command staff, with a department of about 850 members they know just about every individual, hard to believe it but they do. During my first week or so at the GCFES academy, I was sitting in my office working on preparing for the recruit academy. I had no ideal at this point what it was, but then Assistant Chief of Operations Bill Myers came strolling by and poked his head in my office. "Hey Brian, how's everything going?" I was shell shocked to some extent,

I had never personally met him or worked around him. I surely knew who he was but I was so low on the totem pole. Why would he know me? Nevertheless, after the dumbfounded pause I finally said, "It's going great Chief."

The point of the story is that with 850 firefighters it can be easy to get lost in the mix as a firefighter. You could get by with certain things and do a mediocre job and that would be fine. The people that know you would say, "Yeah Brian's a good firefighter and stays out of trouble." However, with the spotlight on only a few people assigned to the Training Division, you do not escape the spot light; in fact it magnifies everything that you do. What you got away with in the field, you will not get away with at the academy and everyone has a few stories. Your bosses and the command staff expect results and they are constantly looking to the academy for innovative and creative solutions to many of the department's issues. The other benefit is that this is your chance to mold the new firefighters entering the fire service. If you want them to do a good job and you want them to truly be firefighters, it requires you to lead by example. Remember, the command staff wants this as well, they do not want to train the new firefighters to cause them problems down the road because of some lack of leadership that they were exposed to in recruit school. Simply put,

> *Attempting to flour someone while in the shower but accidently connecting the coffee cup to said individuals now broke tooth with blood and clumped up flour everywhere may be ok at the station but is an example of what not to attempt at the academy.*

your command staff is going to focus on who is training their department, these are your influencers – your barn bosses.

For me, going to the academy has opened numerous doors that I would never seen in the field. It was a great risk; you never know what is going to happen or where the proverbial yellow brick road may take you. However, you have to make the most of every opportunity given to you and in many situations, you create your own opportunities. In my situation, it has paid me many times over what I have put into it.

When it comes to creating opportunities for yourself, you have to set this up and work at it over your time. The opportunities are endless if you want to do more, but you have to grasp the opportunity when it becomes available. I remember sitting at Station 24 and thinking it would be great to expand outside the bay walls, something in addition to riding the truck every day, which is the greatest job. Riding the truck is some of the greatest times you will ever have (firefighting is the greatest job and the Driver/Engineer is the best position). What I am talking about was sharing something, getting some information out there for others to use or just working on my development skills. So, I set out to write an article for a magazine on Firefighter Health. I worked on it for quite some time and even got the department involved, especially since their program, FireFit Living, was my background. I eventually finished it and sent it through the chain for review, and it came back with the explanation that they were not quite ready to field any questions nationally on the program. Rightfully so, I probably jumped the gun on trying to submit something like that, but it taught me a lot about my company officers and battalion chief at the time (Captain Scott Shepperd and Battalion Chief John Boling). They were more than willing to help and even took the time to proof it more than once for me.

If we move along about 2 years later, I tried my hand at writing again, this time on subjects that I directly had control over and knew intimately myself. My first article was titled, the original, Leadership From the Little Guy. I worked on it, never thinking that it would get picked up by Fire Engineering but it ran about two months later in their e-newsletter. While I was writing it, all I really set out to do was challenge myself (really just to prove all of my high school/college teachers that made me a C student wrong). Simply, I wanted to know if I could accomplish it or not. Now, there is no big risk in this, just submitting an article even if I get turned down. However, there was everything to gain and what I gained personally cannot be put into words. I started to realize at this point that if I wanted it bad enough and worked at it I could get it, no matter what it was. This also happens to be about the same time that I jumped into the driver's seat of the Everyone Goes Home Program for Georgia. There were many changes at this point in my career and since that article I have went on to author over 35 publications, the Training Officer's Toolbox and Managing Editor/Author for the Training Officers Desk Reference by Jones and Bartlett, none of this would be possible without taking risk.

The Buck Doesn't Stop Here

The opportunities did not just stop here for me. I learned that opportunities seem to attract to each other. Motivated people are attracted to motivated crews. For example, when you get around a group of Georgia Smoke Divers or the FLAMES group you can't help but be motivated – it is just the mentality and attitude of the

Let your crews have fun, create a patch/sticker and use it to bring everyone together.

group. So, I started writing about building construction, leadership, generations, fire department economics, and lessons learned from incidents. Each time that I wrote an article something would come with it, something that is very hard to come by and takes time to build. Very similar to respect. I started building credibility from the content of my writing. It is quite awesome when someone from out in Texas sends you an email and says hey I just read your article and it was great. It's not about self-gratification, but you have to admit it is cool when something like that happens. Allow yourself to be challenged by taking risk in order to build credibility; you are validating what you have been taught. Do not be afraid to be wrong, however you must bring your A-Game. I encourage you to find avenues for you to express your thoughts, experiences or lessons learned and allow people to respond – the good and the bad. Take note of the good and study the bad, what was bad, what did the audience feel? Use this information as constructive criticism to make yourself better. And, don't forget those that helped you get there. Chief Bobby Halton and Diane Rothschild took a chance on that first article and many more since then. To date, because they took that chance on me, they are the only publisher that I have ever submitted work too.

I have never asked him and do not know to this day why City of Atlanta Battalion Chief David Rhodes offered me his assistance. However, he did and for the next several years I constantly plagued him with request, articles, and questions. I have no idea why he took the time to offer that to me, a 23-year-old kid (from a different department) that kind of help, but he did. He has since been a great resource for me and I will never be able to pay him back for all that he has done for me. Remember I said the Fire Service was more than willing to help, and Chief Rhodes has done that and more. He is also the same person that introduced me to Gary Klein's research on decision making which made its way into some of my articles and classes. This is just another one of the benefits of Stepping Up and Stepping Out and realizing that the Buck Doesn't Stop Here. If I retired today, there is nothing that I would regret from all of the growth opportunities which I have been able to give back.

Start Your Own Program

GCFES recognized that they wanted to increase the amount of communication between the Chief Officers and the Company Officers, while increasing safety and awareness. In response, they came up with the Officers Forum. Inside this forum, the officers develop short classes based on what they have encountered in the field and teach each other about their experiences and "Best Practices." The program is not mandatory, in fact it's voluntary with no compensation for attending, but strongly encouraged and it has had a tremendous amount of success. A great friend and Co-Hort, Captain Chuck Barnwell ran the program as part of his duties at the Fire Academy. He set up the logistics (facilities and equipment), the speakers, and taught some of it himself. It was easy to maintain once he got started and provided a tremendous amount of knowledge sharing amongst officers. How effective is this program? It is inexpensive (remember, bootstrapping), everybody is involved, and information is being shared that could influence a tremendous amount of lives. Other departments in the area have mimicked this approach and created their own Officers Forum. We even discussed creating an Acting Officers Forum for the "informal leader" level however; the logistics for accomplishing this in an 850-member department is no small feat. This could be much more manageable in smaller departments for the Acting Officers Forum.

Let us move back to the Gut Check Analysis which we discussed earlier. You have Stepped Up to the plate, you have dug your feet in – you just have to swing now. The Stepping Out part can sometimes be affected by several variables. Everyone has heard the saying, "Choose your battles wisely." Here is where you have too, if for whatever reason your department does not support your idea, sometimes you need to drop it and move on. However, if you feel (best to have at least a small group that believes the same as you) that your idea needs to be reviewed more in depth and there are great benefits that can be gained from it, then do it. Find out what their concerns are. Why are they hesitant? Is it money, leadership (not their idea), resources? Find out the answers to all of these without being too aggressive (remember it's about being assertive), at this point it is more important to listen than to talk. Once you have obtained all of the questions, research them and put a specific and honest answer to each. At this point, go back and present the information, being able to answer all of their questions will please them, look impressive, and reduce any myths or misconceptions.

When I created the Gwinnett County Leadership and Safety Conference there were a lot of doubters and hoops to go through. I learned a lot about the dynamics of what goes on at the command staff level. Although I put all of the risk on me, I wanted my

department to be involved in the conference. It took a lot of communicating and explaining why I wanted to do it, who was accepting funds and where would the

2009 Conference

funds be going when it was all over. These were just some of the questions that had to be answered. There were many ideals offered to me some I took and others I did not. Be prepared when you step into something of this nature. I realized early on that I would not be able to do this on my own, and one of our Administrative Staff Associates, Leslie Kalmbach was bribed into helping me. Honestly, she did all of the hard work and deserves all of the credit for both years we did the conference. However, once we got everything rolling and everything was explained to the command staff they jumped on board and we turned out about 250 firefighters from the area to hear some local speakers such as Retired Gwinnett County Fire Chief Steve Rolader and City of Atlanta Fire Chief Kelvin Cochran but also Chief John Norman, Chief Rick Lasky, Chief Eddie Buchanan and Chief John Salka. I thought it was just great that I got to hear them speak, that's all I really wanted. The benefit of developing the conference, which never existed before in Atlanta, and managing the process were added benefits to taking that risk. Could I have failed, absolutely – but I didn't.

Tips For Organizing Your Own Training Event

I received a phone call sitting at Station 11, aka the Tough House, one night from my friend Tom Hancock asking if I could fill him in on what did I do right and what did I do wrong after two years of running the Gwinnett County Leadership and Safety Conference. So, I filled him in on all of the ins and outs which I had learned through just doing it and shortly after our discussion the Metro Atlanta Firefighters Conference (MAFFC) was born. MAFFC has seen tremendous growth the last seven years and well worth any firefighter's time.

Even though the first conference was a huge success, there was a lot of learning that I had to figure out very quickly. If you're interested in putting a training event together but you are not really sure where to start or what all goes into it. Hopefully, these tips and considerations will help you, at least so that you don't feel like you are trying to throw darts in the dark. These tips will apply whether it's a conference, seminar, or just a one day training event. I will say some are easier than others, especially when there is no money or airports involved, however, it is nothing you can't handle. Since the first Gwinnett Conference, I've organized or helped organize numerous events since then and learned something new each time.

Tip #1

Plan early! When I first started looking at the Gwinnett Conference I thought I could pull everything together in three months, approximately 8 months later is what it took. I never dreamed that speakers would be booked a year in advance but a lot are such as Rhodes, Halton, Norman, Gasaway, Buchanan and Lasky. You will have to get them early on, plan for next year's now. This is exactly what we did with the 2nd Gwinnett Conference, I started planning and booking about 11 months before the date.

Tip #2

Get help, now! Don't think that you will be able to handle this on your own, not even the smallest event. If you are the one organizing it, you need to be available 24/7 at least during the conference just in case. Find people that are willing to help, you'll be surprised at how many people would love to get involved. Yeah, some of them just want in for free, but if they're going to work let them, there's nothing wrong with that. But, find your Leslie

Kalmbach, someone you can trust and definitely smarter than me. In addition, speaking generally, you need 2 people for registration, 1 person assigned to help each speaker with their own vehicle for transportation, 1-2 people working the actual conference room for whatever may happen and have 1 or 2 people in your back pocket that are willing to help as soon as you call.

Tip #3

It's usually best to separate the conference and your department as best you can, especially if venders or money is involved. Go to your local bank and tell them what you are doing. They should be able to set you up with an Educational- banking purposes only account. It's very hard for Governments to take and hand out money in a short time period, just another reason to separate them. Obviously, if the department is willing to pay for all of the training and no money will change hands except to the speakers, keep it simple and keep it all in-house.

Tip #4

Advertising is the key. Even after the conference, when I thought everyone was aware I had people mention that they knew nothing about it. Send emails, flyers, and make phone calls to every department, firefighter and chief associations, chiefs meeting, state fire academy, and any website that you can think of. Fire Engineering is more than willing to post any event materials, International Association of Fire Chiefs, FireRescue1.com, and others are just as willing. Also, start a website, you can purchase a domain name and address through Yahoo for about $30 a quater. It's worked perfect for a non-tech savvy guy.

Tip #5

If you will need vendor support to help offset some of the cost of the conference, contact them early as well. They generally plan a year in advance for what training they want to support the following year. Most of your support will come from vendors in the local market, a lot of the manufactures even if local don't get involved at smaller scale training events, at least not financially. Once you get the vendors committed take care of them and try everything possible to keep them happy. You want them to come back and help each year. Jeff and Jason Whidby, Georgia Fire and Rescue Supply, was a tremendous supporter of our conference and more than willing to come back and help. Customer Service!!

As for set up, give them a specific table area such as a 10' x 10'. If you can get skirted tables they look really nice for the vendors. Provide them with free water and if you can - buy their lunch for helping provide the training. Talk to them and see what they have to offer, you may be able to walk away with some cool fire stuff (that shouldn't be your reason why, but a good fringe benefit). As well, offer different amounts of participation and discounts if they register early. Get there name out there for everyone to see. I started the Gwinnett Conference off with a PowerPoint Presentation that had all of their logos, booklets with their logos and brief description, Tshirts, website, and verbal recognition as many times as possible during the conference.

Also, make sure that the vendors bring little items that a firefighter can purchase (if practical), not just the big ticket items for departments.

Tip #6

Create a release of liability form if you have any Hands-on Training. Most understand the training is at their own risk, however; eliminate issues before it escalates. It is also important to each have a safety officer on site and operate similar to a Type III Incident. During one of the Metro Atlanta FOOLs events we operated four Hands-on-Training drills across a 13 acre complex using this very system.

Tip #7

When looking for speakers, some of your greatest speakers may be in your backyard and speak for free. Retired Fire Chief Steve Rolader, Retired Assistant Chief Bill Myers, Retired Assistant Chief Greg Schaffer, and Fire Chief Kelvin Cochran were all free (helps a lot on cost) but were awesome speakers that are more than willing to help and wanted to be involved. Tap into that talent pool. As well, during a Metro Atlanta Fraternal Order of Leatherheads training event, Firefighter Survival Weekend – June 2009; we used all local speakers and instructors. You will be amazed at their willingness to get the information out there. This particular training event was absolutely free for anyone wanting to attend.

Tip #8

Put some art work to it. The art work that is on the website and on the forms came from an advertising agreement with an online publisher. We advertised for them and they wanted to help us advertise and get the information out there. Also, ask people around you that are artist or tech savvy and let them help you; again most will do it for free. Catch the firefighter's eye.

Tip #9

Set an agenda for all of the helpers, include times, who, and where they need to be. This will cut out a lot of confusion and reduce the number of questions that you have to answer during the conference. Also, set up an agenda and schedule for the conference. Allow time for breaks, the speakers usually already have them worked into their presentations, find out what works for them. Remember, the more people you're trying to move the longer it will take to get them back in. Sometimes it's best to take fewer but longer breaks. In addition, make sure that you have enough time for the vendors to interact with the attendees. And by the way, make sure that the vendors are set up so that the attendees have to walk through them to get to the bathroom, classroom, or wherever. Don't assume people will just go to the vendors, make it happen without being pushy.

Tip # 10

Work out a deal with a local venue to host your training, if you're department does not have an auditorium. Our county does but with vendors attending, it may look like favoritism, so it's best to just separate the two. A lot of hotels can hold 150 – 250 people, plus they have restaurants, bars, and the rooms are right there. Our first conference was in a Holiday Inn Select and it had every bit of that. Make sure to work with them and see what options they can give you. Holiday Inn actually gave us the lecture room for free, as long as I raised $2,200 dollars a day for their catering service (this price will vary by vendor). I paid for them to feed us and we got the room for free. However, the second year we rented the Civic Center due to the increased numbers of firefighters attending, around 300.

Also, make sure to get discounted hotel rates. If you're at the venue, such as Holiday Inn, get a good rate for your attendees, they can also compensate you a free room if you book so many. Our agreement was 1 free room for the speakers per 25 sold. It's not a lot but it's something. If you're working with somewhere like a civic center, they generally already have agreements with the nearby hotels.

Tip #11

You don't have to try and make money. One of the reasons for engaging vendors is so you can offset the cost of the conference/seminar so the average firefighter can attend. Our first year, we had pretty good vendor involvement; I believe it was around 10 or so, and we had extra money at the end. This dilemma is good and bad. The bad is that we could have made it more affordable to the firefighters, even though it was only $150 for the 3 days and their lunch was included, not too bad for the caliber of speakers that we had. However, the good was that we were able to donate it to some very worthy non-profits. We donated $3,000 to both, the Metro Atlanta Fire Chiefs Association for future Metro Atlanta training and the Gwinnett County Firefighters Benevolent Fund to take care of our firefighters and their families. The other option, if you know that you're going to do it again, is to keep it so that you have something to start with for next year. We just choose to donate our proceeds.

Tip #12

The final tip, make sure that you send out all of the registration information to the attendees about 4 months in advance. Good free training can usually be turned around fairly quickly; generally it's not a problem. When we sent out the Metro Atlanta FOOLS training event I received the first registration within I believe 15 minutes. However, the more that it cost the sooner it needs to be out there. Generally, a firefighter will think about it for a month, look at scheduling time off the next month, register the following month, and attend the next month. They may also need reminders. It's something that they want to do; they just have a million other things going on like everyone else. With that being said, think about the late comers, with the Gwinnett Conference, we had

30 or more people want to register the week of. Make it happen if you have the room, it's about taking care of each other.

Wrapping Up

These tips should be able to set you on your way and give you a few considerations to think as you plan your training event. I will say that it is much more cost effective to bring speakers in for your department than it is to send everyone out to the extremely large conferences. Now, with saying that there is a lot to gain from attending these large conferences, such as Fire Department Instructors Conference (FDIC). I attend FDIC every year to learn, to network with other firefighters and to work with potential vendors. Almost half of the vendor money that we received came from contacts that I made at conferences like FDIC.

Key Points

- Do what is right.

- Believe in Truth, Trust, Respect and Unity or develop your own core values.

- Think outside of I-285.

- Step Up and Step Out, and create your own program.

- Remember to communicate, and timing is everything when starting a project even if it will save lives. Remember to bootstrap it.

- Step Up and Step Out even if some are afraid to or have never tried it before. Remember, the buck doesn't just stop here, it keeps going. So, take the risk, you won't regret it.

- Make sure it comes from your heart.

Chapter 5

"To lead people, walk behind them."

Lao Tzu

What's Behind the Badge?

Has anyone ever told you what it means to wear the badge, or what the Maltese Cross means, or where did it even come from? The Maltese Cross is what we are, each point on the cross stands for something that exemplifies what it means be to a firefighter. If we forget what it means or do not share with each other what it means to wear the badge, then how do we know what we stand for, or maybe we will just forget our history, our tradition. We have to study our history so we know where we came from, in essence, so we know where it is that we are going. One of the strongest aspects of a leader is the aspect of remembering where they came from and setting a vision forward.

The Story of the Maltese Cross

This story is hundreds of years old:

When a courageous band of crusaders known as The Knights of St. John fought the Saracens for possession of the holy land, they encountered a new weapon unknown to European warriors. It was a simple, but horrible device of war. It brought excruciating pain and agonizing death upon the brave fighters for the cross.

As the crusaders advanced on the walls of the city, they were struck by glass bombs containing naphtha. When they became saturated with the highly flammable liquid, the Saracens would hurl a flaming torch into their midst. Hundreds of the knights were burned alive; others risked their lives to save their brothers-in-arms from dying painful, fiery deaths.

Thus, these men became our first Firefighters and the first of a long list of courageous men and women. Their heroic efforts were recognized by fellow crusaders who awarded each hero a badge of honor – a cross, similar to the one firefighters wear today. Since the Knights of St. John lived for close to four centuries on a little island in the Mediterranean Sea named Malta, the cross became known as the Maltese Cross.

The Maltese Cross is our symbol of protection. It means that the Firefighter who wears this cross is willing to lay down his or her life for you just as the crusaders sacrificed their lives for their family so many years ago. The Maltese Cross is a Firefighter's badge of honor, signifying that they work in courage – a ladder's rung away from death.

This is where it all started before there were two stage pumps, PPE, or SCBA's. This is where the courage that is expected of firefighters today comes from. This is important to know for many reasons, laying down a life to protect another is nothing new; we have being doing it for hundreds of years. This is where the Brotherhood started, what it stands for, and we should never forget it.

Points of the Cross

This story was where the cross came from and why it was given. Now, within the cross there are several meanings, eight to be specific. There are 8 points on a Maltese Cross, so there are 8 meanings within the cross. If you research this material you may find slightly different meanings or sayings but to the best of my research I have put in this book what I believe is the truth. The first list of eight is described as being obligations that the knights had to commit to and live by. This also happens to be a good list of core values for firefighters to live by.

1. live in truth;
2. have faith;
3. repent of sins;
4. give proof of humility;
5. love justice;
6. be merciful;
7. be sincere and whole-hearted; and
8. endure persecution.

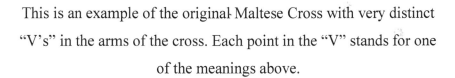

This is an example of the original Maltese Cross with very distinct "V's" in the arms of the cross. Each point in the "V" stands for one of the meanings above.

Modern Maltese Cross

The modern day Maltese Cross has slightly different meaning but there are still 8 points that represent the cross. They are:

1. Gallantry
2. Sympathy
3. Tact
4. Observation
5. Perseverance
6. Loyalty
7. Explicitness
8. Dexterity

Gallantry   Perseverance
Sympathy   Loyalty
Tact   Dexterity
Observation   Explicitness

This is an example of the modern day Maltese Cross and the 8 meanings corresponding with the 8 points.

We should at least know that these words and meanings exist. This is something that should be stressed in every fire station but also in the recruit schools as these firefighters are joining our family. Let them know up front what they are getting into and what it means to wear this badge. There are organizations and companies across the world that would die for the marketing image of the fire department. The problem is they cannot and will never understand what it means to live by the meaning of the points on the cross. So, here is the meaning to which we should try to live by:

Gallantry means showing spirited and conspicuous bravery or an act of marked courtesy. Be courteous to everyone, and when the time comes to save a life be unwavering in your commitment.

Sympathy is the act or capacity of entering into or sharing the feelings or interests of another. Sometimes its referred to as the feeling or mental state brought about by sensitivity. We have to show concern and care for our patients and each other.

Perseverance means to persist in a state or undertaking in spite of counterinfluences, opposition, or discouragement. Hanging in there, and having HEART!

Loyalty means being faithful to a cause, ideal, custom, institution, or product. Be loyal to the service, your department, and to your core values.

Tact is using a keen sense of what to do or say in order to maintain good relations with others or avoid offense. Be kind to everyone.

Observation is watching carefully; especially paying attention to details or a behavior for the purpose of arriving at a judgment that could save someone's life. Not being aware of our surroundings is one of the biggest killers of firefighters.

Dexterity means having the skills to perform, being ready to perform and performing with grace. This means that we have to train to the point where our skills function as if they are part of our bodies, not just a firefighter and their tool.

Explicitness means fully revealing or expressing without vagueness, implication, or ambiguity: leaving no question as to meaning or intent. Be decisive, especially on the fire ground, one of the worst things that an individual can do in most cases is to do nothing at all and once you've made a decision, make your message clear and concise.

The Star of Life

With the Fire Services role ever expanding to take care of the public that we serve and similar to many departments it is a requirement to be a first responder, EMT, or paramedic; we should know about the Star of Life as well. Within the Fire Service, those of us that run EMS know that 60%-80% of our calls are EMS related. The Star of Life does not have the history and tradition of the Maltese Cross but that doesn't make it any less important. We should understand it and live by it just as well.

Where did the Star of Life come from?

It was designed by Leo R. Schwartz, Chief of the EMS Branch, National Highway Traffic Safety Administration (NHTSA). It was created after the American National Red Cross complained in 1973 that they objected to the common use of an Omaha orange cross on a square background of reflectorized white, which clearly imitated the Red Cross symbol. NHTSA investigated this concern, felt the complaint was justified and set out to design a symbol suited for EMS.

The newly designed, six barred cross, was adopted from the Medical Identification Symbol of the American Medical Association and was registered as a certification mark on February 1, 1977 with the Commissioner of Patents and Trade-marks in the name of the National Highway Traffic Safety and Administration.

Each of the bars of the blue "Star of Life" represents the six system functions of EMS, as illustrated below. Each bar represents an aspect of what we do when the call comes in, but it also represents the patient's life cycle through this emergency call. We have the obligation to know our materials, and to be good at our job so that we can *detect* what their concerns are about. We need to be able to clearly, concisely *report* to the ER what we have encountered. We have the responsibility to *respond* in an appropriate manner, arriving alive. Our *on scene care* has a lot to do with our external customer service skills, we should be genuinely concerned about the patient and doing everything possible to help them. The *care in transit* that we give is also part of our customer service, but it's also part of continuing our assessment and trying to remedy their illness. As well, we have the responsibility to make sure that the patient is transferred to *definitive care* quickly but in an appropriate manner which keeps them safe and for us to not be negligent.

As you can see the Star of Life represents a patient's life cycle through their time of need. I understand that it's hard at times, especially at 2 in the morning running a toe cramp, that started 3 weeks ago but, we still have to provide the same level of care. I remember very clearly riding the Med Unit at Station 14 and 15 (specifically) and the frequent flyers that we had. Station 15 Med Unit was coined as the "place where dreams go to die." It was not always nice and it surely was not always pretty but they needed us and we delivered. You should also remember these are the same people that are voting on whether we keep a job or get that new station. There's a comment at the bottom of every email that Retired Chief Steve Rolader sends out. It simply says, "We don't define the service, we provide the service."

The Snake

The snake and staff in the center of the symbol portray the staff of Asclepius who, according to Greek mythology, was the son of Apollo (god of light, truth and prophecy). Supposedly, Asclepius learned the art of healing from the centaur Chiron; but Apollo's father – king of the gods, was fearful that because of the Asclepius knowledge, all men might be rendered immortal. Rather than have this occur, Zeus slew Asclepius with a thunderbolt. Later, Asclepius was worshipped as a god and people slept in his temples, as it was rumored that he affected cures of prescribed remedies to the sick during their dreams. Eventually, Zeus restored Asclepius to life, making him a god.

Asclepius was usually shown in a standing position, dressed in a long cloak, holding a staff with a serpent coiled around it. The staff has since come to represent medicine's only symbol. In the Caduceus, used by physicians and the Military Medical Corp., the staff is winged and has two serpents intertwined. Even though this does not hold any medical relevance in origin, it represents the magic wand of the Greek deity, Hermes, messenger of the gods.

The staff with the single serpent is the symbol for Medicine and Health and the winged staff is the symbol for peace. The Staff with the single serpent represents the time when Asclepius had a very difficult patient that he could not cure, so he consulted a snake for advice and the patient survived. The snake had coiled around Asclepius's staff in order to be head to head with him as an equal when talking. The Winged staff came about when Mercury saw two serpents fighting, and unable to stop them any other way placed his staff between them causing them to coil up his winged staff.

As well from historical perspective the Bible, Numbers 21:9, makes reference to a serpent on a staff: "Moses accordingly made a bronze serpent and mounted it on a pole and whenever anyone who had been bitten by a serpent looked at the bronze serpent, he recovered from the snake bite." Considering everything we have discussed this chapter, there is a very intriguing history behind the fire service and EMS.

U.S. Based Fire History

Firehistory.org based out of Summerville (SC) has numerous articles on fire service history of the United States and I would encourage you to look them up. Understanding the fire service history will also teach you about why we have certain codes, standards and laws.

New London School Explosion

New London, Texas, 1937, an undetected natural gas leak accumulated in the schools crawl space and exploded killing 296 children and staff. Texas mandated that mercaptan be added to natural gas for detection purposes. Mercaptan is what you smell today in natural gas.

Iroquois Theatre Fire

Chicago, Illinois, 1903, hot stage lights ignited a velvet curtain used as a backdrop for the play resulting in 602 fire related fatalities. There were no automatic sprinklers, the stage fire curtain did not close properly, no smoke vents and many of the exit doors either were locked or did not swing in the direction of travel.

Our Lady of the Angels School Fire

Chicago, Illinois, 1958, a fire in a cardboard trash can in a basement stairwell ignited. The fire spread through the combustible wall and ceiling in the exit corridors. There were no automatic sprinklers, no automatic fire alarms and the exit stairway was unenclosed. 92 children and three teachers perished.

Winecoff Hotel Fire

Atlanta, Georgia, 1946, a fire quickly spread throughout the upper floors of the hotel causing many people to jump to their death. There was only one escape route for the upper floors which the fire spread through due to doors being propped open. There was no sprinkler system and no fire alarm system. 119 fatalities – deadliest hotel fire in the United States. If you read inside the front cover of the NFPA 101 Life Safety Code Book the Winecoff Hotel Fire is specifically stated as a reason for the codes existence – I learned this by diversifying from the fire department operations sector and attended an inspections class to broaden my horizons.

Other fires to research:

- Hackensack, New Jersey Bowstring Trusses
- Kingsman, Arizona BLEVE
- Boston Vendome Hotel Collapse
- Hartford Circus Fire
- Cocoanut Grove Nightclub Fire
- MGM Grand Hotel Fire
- New York Black Sunday
- Yarnell Hill 19

Learn the Historical Perspectives

I'm sure that you have heard the saying "those which do not learn from the past are doomed to repeat it." There are many other aspects of the fire services history that are worth mentioning, however it is beyond the scope of this text.

"Those which do not learn from the past are deemed to repeat it."

During my involvement with the ISFSI/NIST Burns in Spartanburg, South Carolina I was introduced to the name Lloyd Layman by Chief Shane Ray. In order to understand the historical importance of Chief Layman ask yourself these questions:

> Do you understand the broken pattern for droplets of water when using a nozzle?

> Do you understand compartmentalization and the effects of steam conversion?

> Do you know what the fog nozzle was designed for?

Lloyd Layman is known as the father of the fog and was originally a naval officer who brought his naval shipboard firefighting techniques to the mainstream. During the 1950's Layman wrote many books and presented at FDIC "Little Droplets of Water." He explained what we are talking about today, 50 years later, with the Principles of Modern Fire Attack with the International Society of Fire Service Instructors. The question you are forced to ask then, if Chief Layman was teaching these practices in the 1950's why are we learning this all over again.

There are a couple of reasons in my opinion:

> #1: We do not study enough history to understand the impacts of when we make changes to our equipment or practices. The fog nozzle was never designed to do what the

modern fire service has adapted it to be. At the same time we pushed the gear manufacturers to improve our PPE without changing our tactical considerations. We failed to understand the historical perspective and how all of these items fit together. As gear improved we went further into the structures with the same fog nozzle that was designed to be used from the exterior of the fire room in order to steam out the fire.

#2: Chief Layman's knowledge was based mainly on experience as we did not have the science available that we currently have today, thanks to organizations such as the International Society of Fire Service Instructors, National Institute of Standards and Technology, and Underwriters Laboratories. We now have the science to assist in explaining fire behavior and various water applications. Tying in the historical perspectives with the current science and technology is vital. Attempting to use past techniques and not understanding why/how it was designed can be dangerous.

Other historical applications that you should research include the items below. Most of us use one or the other applications during pre-plans, however, not understanding the intent may be mis-leading. Ed Hartin does an amazing job capturing the historical perspective and the development of both formulas. I encourage you to visit www.CFTB-US.com and read both of these articles so that the next time you do a pre-plan you understand why you are using these formulas.

National Fire Academy Fire Flow Formula – Developed in 1980 at the National Fire Academy by an expert panel based on typical fire ground responses. This was strictly based on the experiences of this staff. Ed Hartin describes the use of the NFA Formula as being intended for estimating the total flow rate required when making a direct attack and has a number of specific parameters that must be considered.

Iowa State Fire Flow Formula – Based on research and empirical evidence in 1950's by Keith Royer and Floyd W. (Bill) Nelson. They identified the volume and water flow need for fire control using a fog nozzle. Ed Hartin describes the formula on his website CFTB-US.com as "The Iowa Rate of Flow Formula is designed to estimate the flow rate required to control a fire in a single open area of a building with a 30 second application of water fog. This approach requires foreknowledge of the building and made the Iowa rate of flow formula most suited for preplanning, rather than tactical application."

Original Water Main   **Ladder Truck**

Dispatch Board – All
photos taken at the
Maryland Fire Museum in
Baltimore, Maryland

Key Points

- Learn about where you came from. Why do we wear the
  badge and what does it mean?
- Remember the sacrifice that the first firefighters made for
  their fallen comrades.
- Live by the 8 points of the Maltese Cross.
- Live by the Star of Life and consider the patient's life cycle
  through their time of need.
- Remember, we are a servant to the public, we provide what
  the citizens ask of us. As, Retired Chief Rolader stated, "We
  don't define the service, we provide the service."

Chapter 6

"Outstanding leaders go out of their way to boost the self-esteem of their personnel. If people believe in themselves, it's amazing what they can accomplish."

Sam Walton

Keep Your Head About It!

In order to have long-term success in any organization every individual has to establish a level of credibility amongst his or her peers. The presence of this credibility will

"Where in your expectations is your crew operating?"

determine your ability to navigate the organization to include urgency of work completed, decision making ability, office politics and team trust. The ability of your team to understand your sense of urgency sets the tone for how the work should be handled. On a daily basis I receive status reports which discuss various operational expectations that I have previously discussed with my team. From time to time, my team will document that we are outside of our parameters/expectations and they will notate why we are and what they have done to mitigate the circumstance – where in your expectations is your crew operating? In the beginning, the culture was not always operating within expectations. There was a road traveled to get to this point in time, at first nothing was being reported so we had to alter the behavior of what is considered acceptable and this is not the troops fault. The first step is to understand what is important to your team and what do they understand about the chosen expectations. Sure, it would be easy to create a policy or bring down a decision, however, if they do not understand why we want to perform a task a certain way there will be no sense of urgency to complete it, if it gets completed at all Discussing this with your team may enlighten you to other obstacles or difficulties not previously considered. The second step was to educate my team on the importance of these expectations, detailing the implications of each expectation whether it is a cost, safety, environmental, or an efficiency factor. The third step is to set the expectations with the team. This step allows you to discuss your expectations but also allows for any questioning and answering that may be required. In addition to setting the expectations for your team you must teach their firefighters what is required and why. This step will provide a couple of benefits:

1) It will streamline the message to the organization, reducing the amount of time it will take to effectively implement.

2) It will eliminate a large majority of misconceptions/rumors/uncertainties.

3) It will eliminate your subordinates being put into an awkward situation of having to justify or modify a decision based on the lower level employee not understanding the expectation.

4) It will allow for a more cohesive unit (for example, if I know the end of the shift expectations I do not have to wait to be told to complete it as I should handle it when I see it).

Real Life Stuff: Recently, I received a text from a fellow brother in a different part of the country where I had presented a few months back with the words "I'm looking for inspiration, I've lost my motivation from the decisions being made by our officers." He went on to discuss the morale of the department and it had nothing to do with actions on the fire ground, state of the equipment or money. The morale had been pushed down from a lack of understanding and communication between the brass and the troops on day to day operational stuff. He provided a few examples where he stated he simply did not understand how the decision was derived. If the brass would take the three steps above and take the time to communicate with their troops they create a bond and trust amongst each other. There are many times when I did not understand the decisions being made but when I make these decisions now I make it point to explain to the crews why we are doing what we do. As I replied back to by brother: "Your motivation is a direct reflection of you and no one can change that but you. If morale is low, now is the time that the group needs a leader more than ever to pull everyone together. This is when true character stands out." However, all of this could have potentially been avoided from creating a common understanding.

When this approach is taken, it allows your co-workers to understand your point of reference, your concerns, they know that their concerns were listened to and they understand the sense of urgency required. This due process will build your credibility with your co-workers and they will learn what to expect from you.

Once the expectations of the organization are understood, you start to build the unity/cohesiveness amongst the leadership group and mentality is pointed in a common direction. The key here is to start to allow your subordinates to make their own decisions. As employees gain technical competence (knowledge and skills, and the why) and they are given a point of reference to make decisions, they should be allowed to exercise these rights. In

> *"The abilities of your subordinates is developed through training, experience and pre/post incident critiques."*

essence, they have earned their decision rights and just as we earn the rights, they can be removed. The military uses a very similar approach known as the Intent of Command. The United States Warfighting Doctrine explains the process as when the Commanding Officer (CO) describes the situation at hand and then discusses implications, contraindications, and desired outcome. In essence, the CO is setting the vision and allowing the subordinates to carry out the mission. The end result is that the mission should be executed within the parameters established, however the key here is that many times we do not have the time to call the next in line leader and ask for a decision to be made. The subordinates need to understand the expectations and the desired outcome so that they can make the decision as soon as the situation arises. The abilities of your subordinates is developed through training, experience and pre/post incident critiques. Leaders should not underestimate the power of sitting down with your co-workers in an informal manner and discussing situations pre and post incident. The Barn Boss should lead this process.

Case Study

When I developed the Emergency Organization for one industrial facility, the challenges included no industrial rescue experience and limited knowledge from volunteer firefighters in their hometowns which were employees of the organization. However, they ran 24 hours per day, 7 days a week and I knew that it was unrealistic for one or two individuals to be there every hour. Furthermore, in reality, if they waited for a response from me for every situation, the outcome would more than likely not be a favorable situation. In order to combat this situation I followed these steps:

1) A discussion was held with all selected Emergency Organization team members prior to any training taking place. We discussed the path forward, the reasons why and the desired outcome. This allowed them to develop a frame of mind concerning the expectations.

2) Extensive training took place to include in-house qualifications and outside certifications. During this first round of qualifications and outside certifications I found it important to join my employees each and every day, completing the

training the same as they did. I trusted my "newly trained" employees to raise and lower me alongside a five story wall. This gave them confidence in their skills and abilities.

3) After the training I sat down with my newly formed team and discussed the standard operating procedures and my expectations. Any final questions and concerns were brought up and then we executed the plan. In the beginning there were several situations where I was called and asked to make the decision of non-life threatening situations, however, after some coaching and time working with the employees these calls disappeared. Furthermore, after six months of this team being in place the table was completely turned as I would walk on the floor and they would tell me what they were doing from a proactive standpoint and what resources they needed.

This was the transitioning to a new Barn Boss, as I relinquished my Barn Boss status and moved up the chain, I had developed Barn Bosses to take my place – share your knowledge.

One of the most difficult and demoralizing issues that can arise is conflict within the organization or "station politics." Usually this is derived from someone who is not able to rationalize a situation and has developed their own decision prior to hearing any alternatives or they have their own agenda. The issue here is that progress is halted until the group is able to reach a common place. Having that high level of credibility will assist in combating these situations in many cases (not all). If your peers understand your point of reference, believe that your true intent has always been what is best for the organization, and you have always provided due diligence to your decisions you will have a much better time working toward that common ground. Great communication skills, understanding human behavior, generational differences and the ability to relate to one another are all major components of working towards a common goal.

We discussed team trust earlier in this chapter. We mention it here simply to tie it back in to relate its importance in leadership. If your employees trust you and you trust them there is a sense of mutual respect and understanding that each of you know your roles and expectations. The ability to build these traits and develop them over time will prove well for development of credibility of you and your team, which goes right back to the discussion around implicit communication.

One of the simplest actions you can take to keep the credibility and recognition that you have gained is to keep it from going to your head. I am a big advocate of furthering your training and education, especially in Georgia, where we have two great offerings. Due to the lottery funds, Georgia has a HOPE Scholarship program that will pay a good amount if not all of your college tuition so there is no reason for someone to not further their education from a cost standpoint. Furthering your knowledge and working to understand the science of fire beyond the one day fire behavior class you get in recruit school should have great emphasis. Having a degree is a significant accomplishment, I have one but a college degree and .50 cent at the local waffle house can get you a cup of coffee. You must take the experiences, lessons learned and the resources that you took away from your studies and use them to make your department, region and state better; that's when it matters.

During the 2009 Gwinnett County Leadership and Safety Conference in Atlanta, Chief Kelvin Cochran conducted a presentation titled Developing Authentic Leadership. His point in the presentation was that there are numerous methods and routes to take with being a good leader, but the key is to develop your leadership to fit you and the people that you work with. He also went on to say that sometimes we move to fast with trying to get every certification and build the impressive portfolio that rivals any Fire Chief before the firefighter can even drive an apparatus. It was impressive to hear him name every certification and degree level known to the fire service, without taking a breath.

However, I agree and disagree with his take on it. If you're constantly working towards trying to be a better firefighter and you're looking for ways to improve the efficiency and effectiveness of your Knowledge, Skills, and Abilities, then why not take every class that you can get into. You're not doing it for money, fame or recognition; you're doing it for the brotherhood. Every day we have to be a student of the Fire Service. I have tried to put my hands on every tool that I can, with the thought that it's a tool that I put away in my toolbox until I need it. Even if it is 10 years down the road when I pull the tool out, the tool is still there.

Now, with what Chief Cochran said and the part that I agree with. If you're out there just trying to build a resume and don't really have your heart in it, you don't need it. If you're a CFO and EFO with only 4 years of experience in the service, why did you get it? Are you simply trying to jump ship or have you done anything with it? Honestly, there's not a huge demand right now for CFO/EFO/AAS/BS/Ph.D/Dr tailboard firefighters. I'm simply saying if you get, then use it for the right reasons – take on the hard assignments.

The second offering that Georgia provides is the Georgia Smoke Divers Program. This program, while not for everyone, provides a great deal of knowledge, experience and training to any firefighter willing to put themselves up to the task. As I prepared for the qualification testing in order to be accepted into the class I bettered myself every day through gear acclimation and putting my hands on tools every day. The six months of work prior to the test and then two months between the test and the actual class was where you perfected discipline, mental toughness, and grit. The Smoke Diver Instructors provided every answer to successfully complete the course but at the end of the day it is your ability to adapt to the task at hand. This course worked on advancing your knowledge and skills, however, it worked more in depth with decision making and the perfection of the skills you already have. When you are faced with a situation with limited knowledge and you have seconds to make a decision with the potential to save or injure another individual's life – how do you make it? These are the types of teachings that the Smoke Diver Program deliver. The lessons assist you in building your slide tray of experience in order to give you a mental cue when faced with a similar situation in the future. There is a minimum cost, but a lifetime of experiences, and, ah yes – the coveted Black T-Shirt (picture on below – I just completed the final drill and crossed over to the other side). For all of my GSD Cods – What is the Good Word?

They'll Tell You

As you move through your career and you receive these certifications, awards and recognition stay humble about it. This is

tricky because you can't call yourself humble; being humble has to come from the people around, the ones that work with you day in and day out. When they say that you're humble, that's when you know. If you're calling yourself humble, then you're probably not as humble as you think. Most firefighters will tell you when you're being either a jack, suck, dumb- #$#, etc…. Sadly, for the most part if they tell you that, it probably is true. There are some that you don't need to worry about, they'll harass rocks just to pass time. But when this comes from certain people in your department you know there is some truth to it. If you hear it from one of these individuals take it as constructive criticism and see what you can do to change it.

Sometimes you will never see or think that these individuals are just taking your words or actions wrong, but there may just be some truth to it. There was one incident where an engine company came up to the fire academy to complete some live fire burns with the academy staff and a certain lieutenant from the academy saw a separation between a firefighter and his crew. The lieutenant knew the firefighter, his ways from recruit school and decided to talk to the firefighter based on this separation he was seeing. Lieutenant told him that some of the crew felt that he was possibly trying to undermine them with asking questions, when he felt the firefighter simply was just trying to throw out ideals. And sometimes he may come off as if he knew more than the others when he was just trying to help with a situation. The Lieutenant explained to him that a lot of this can be taken care of by simply learning to communicate using tact with the crew. If an outsider such as this can see the separation between crew members then it probably is real. The firefighter took the lieutenants advice and used it to make a difference with how he was perceived by other firefighters. Fast forward several months and the same engine company arrives at the fire academy with a much different cohesiveness. The lieutenant's point of view was correct. If you are the lieutenant here, remember it does not have to be a gripe session about what the firefighter is doing but a more informal and inquisitive approach. I would start off by saying "what do you think" or "have you seen this?" Something to this effect allows the conversation to be open minded and allows the other individual to express his or her concerns without being threatened. A lot of times the message or purpose gets lost due to how it was said or expressed. About 6 months after this heart-to-heart, the firefighter came back and thanked the lieutenant for the talk; he never realized what he was doing.

Tips for Being Humble

Like I mentioned earlier being humble has to be recognized and felt by the people that you work day in and day out with. You cannot proclaim your humbleness, those around you have to. However, there are some things that you can do to yourself to be humble, and helps keep yourself in check a lot of times. Some of these things are as simply as volunteering your time, don't tell everyone how good you are, and go out of your way sometimes to make a difference. Barn Bosses are excellent at this.

#1 It's Not All About You

Early on, one of the first programs that I helped create with Chief Wayne Mooney was the departments Incident Safety Officer Program. You're taught in all the instructor classes that you always put a title page in the presentation, put your contact information on the board and have that credibility statement at the beginning to tell the audience why they should listen to you.

"The Fewer the Words, the Louder the Volume."

These vary tremendously with the crowd or audience which you are presenting to, and you don't always need it. As we started teaching these first classes to extremely higher ranking individuals than me, I tried this format. It's very hard to tell a captain or chief in your department why they need to listen to a "Little Guy," and sometimes you can go overboard with your credibility. You can use it too much. Instead of death by PowerPoint, it's death by credibility. The Fewer the Words, the Louder the Volume.

One day, an outstanding officer that I owe a lot to, Captain Pete, told me, "You know that you don't need your name up on the title page, everyone in here knows who you are already." Huh, what a concept, your department knows who you are – this is the difference between textbook and practicality. What he meant was let the message be your credibility, not your title or status. This same philosophy was carried back to the station floor – let your actions speak for themselves.

#2 Speak Softly and Carry a Big Stick (Theodore Roosevelt)

Be slow to speak in most cases, however, always be prepared too if necessary. I mentioned earlier what Matt Cook mentioned to me about talking and being able to teach. Well, during my first two or three years in the service I was basically scared to talk or even sit down when everyone else was sleeping. I tried very hard to not make the wrong impression, by speaking to often or speaking when I didn't know what I was talking about. It's very similar to crying wolf, if you cry every chance you get people will tend to not listen to you even when the content of the message is well-meant and has a purpose. But, when you speak seldom and know what you are talking about, hence carrying a big stick, people will tend to listen when you do have something to say. This is because they know what you are saying has some merit behind it and you are not just trying to cause disruption every chance you get.

#3 Be Honest About Yourself

We talked about having the college degrees and certifications, etc... I've got the fire officer, instructor, college degree, etc... This is extremely scary, that they will just give these to anyone, however, I'm still no smarter than that rock you just skipped across the water. So, I found it very important to realize my limitations and to know my boundaries within my department and my crew. If you don't know something, admit it, and then attempt to find the correct answer. It's immeasurable how important this trait is for the Barn Boss. For me though, I try to surround myself with good people, which know more and can do more than me. I did this even as a firefighter, even though you can't pick your crew, stay with the ones that know what is going on. I have never been the top athlete or valedictorian but what I lacked in these two categories I tried to make up for in heart and effort.

#4 Volunteer Some Time

Starting from the ground level is usually a good place. As you're trying to learn more about your department and the service, volunteer to help out with some projects. Most of the work that I have done in developing classes and the conference for my department didn't come down as mandates. It was usually something that I saw we could benefit from and I worked on it after hours a lot of the time. It is a lot of work but it's great to see what can happen when you put a little effort into something. Ironically enough, the very day in the MAFCA meeting when I donated the conference proceeds, the chiefs voted on paying two mortgage payments for a family where the husband died in the line-of-duty in South Georgia training from a cardiac arrest - God at Work. These people had never met this family and had no idea that I was about to give this check to them. However, they passed the vote to pay for the mortgages and then received a check from our conference proceeds right behind the vote. That's the true meaning of unity and brotherhood in the Fire Service.

This is just like helping out with the Everyone Goes Home Program, 99% of the people involved are volunteers. They spend time away from home teaching the Courage to be Safe Class, bring attention to the 16 Life Safety Initiatives and meeting with other advocates about how to make the program better. This is stuff that they don't get paid for but yet they do. They volunteer their time because they care. The two others groups I mentioned earlier, Georgia Smoke Divers and FLAMES, all of their instructors offer their time with no compensation. These two classes require 40+ instructors for each day to be successful. While I unfortunately do not attend near as much as I should I am grateful for those that do and carry on the legacy.

These were just a few things that you can do to show how much you appreciate the Fire Service and to show your humbleness. The simple fact is that if you have these kinds of traits and these are the types of things that you are doing people know where your heart is and that is what makes you humble. Retired Fire Phoenix Chief Alan Brunacini offered the following Power Goofs of Bosses in his June 2015 Fire Engineering article *"More Power Goofs."* I encourage you to read them and consider where you stand – there are many you are probably doing right but which can you be better at? This is not the entire list, just a few I picked out.

Power Goofs of Bosses

- The kiss up/kick down.
- They steal, hoard and mismanage credit, continually inflating their own performance/status.
- They possess the uncontrollable urge to unnecessarily "fix," change or alter things by adding their "fingerprints" on them.
- They automatically say, "I" / "me" / "mine" in every statement about anything positive (the "I" person).
- They confuse monologue (me lecturing) with dialogue (us conversing).
- They play goofy information games (information is power) and manipulate information in a self-serving way.

- They practice cronyism: allocate resources, assignments, and projects based on politically motivated friend/enemy, insider/outside, okay/not okay relationships.
- They are aloof and unapproachable.
- They create organizational fear as a control measure.
- They do not understand the dynamics of feelings, they are emotionally illiterate.
- They are poor listeners.
- Their ego has partially or completely eaten their brain.

Key Points

- Don't let any of your accomplishments or awards go to your head. There numerous other people who could achieve the same objectives, don't make yourself an outcast.

- Be motivated, push for great things and further your education and experiences; but do it for the right reasons. Not just because you're trying to build a resume, do it because you want to make this a better service.

- Be humble.

- Work on listening and two-way communication.

- Remember the tips to help you be humble:
  - It's not all about you
  - Speak softly and carry a big stick
  - Be honest about yourself
  - Volunteer some time

Chapter 7

"Leadership is a potent combination of strategy and character. But if you must be without one, be without the strategy."

Norman Schwarzkopf

Leadership vs. Followership

This particular morning was like any other except I happened to be at home instead of work, waiting on the AC Repairman. I awoke about 0630 to go for my morning run as a fire call came in with an address one road down from my residence in the small town where I volunteer. In this volunteer department I am a firefighter at rank and I follow orders instead of the typical giving of them in my career status. While I do not shy away from speaking up, I feel it is important to listen and be respectful with my rookie status (which is kind of fun to say – makes me feel younger). This understanding of leadership versus followership is important to understand as this incident unfolds.

The neighbor stated he believed he sees smoke inside the residence but no one is home. I skipped my morning run and went enroute to the call approximately half a mile away. As I turned down the road I did not see any columns of smoke and for all I knew this would be a quick wash down or false alarm. As I got closer to the address stated by dispatch I still did not see any indication of fire. All of a sudden, in a bend in the middle of the road was the mailbox I was looking for, quickly I looked to my right and saw a lite wisp of black laminar smoke pushing from a small utility room window on Side A. I had arrived first on scene, established command, provided my size up, and conducted my walk around. It was a two story wood frame single family dwelling with smoke showing from the A/D corner on the first floor. As I made my walk around there were no lights on, all doors were locked and no other signs of fire or smoke showing.

As I started back up the hill towards the road an additional volunteer showed up and the two career firefighters on E2 and E3 were seconds later. We immediately exchanged information and transferred command and I rolled back to my firefighter status. One of the firefighters and myself grabbed the 200' 1.75" pre-connect and took off to the front door. I used my rookie status to take over the nozzle. We forced entry into the residence, controlling the flow path and not allowing uncoordinated ventilation. As we forced the front door the smoke quickly leveled itself one foot off the floor at the door and five feet in there was zero visibility.

We continued performing a search along the right hand wall, which would lead us to the A/D corner, looking for a door or hallway. After feeling around some furniture and about 20' in we found a door way and made entry. There was small sense of environmental changes but nothing to alarming, however, we were definitely closer. After about another foot or two I could hear a crackling but I could still not see anything. I made entry into the bed room and felt a definite rush of heat but still could not see any fire. I made the decision to quickly discharge my 150 GPM nozzle into the ceiling to cool the environment but careful to not upset the thermal layering. After a few seconds, the heat did dissipate but I still could not see the fire in these less than ideal conditions. These are the ones that scare me the most or maybe you just call it being respectful -

you hear it, see the smoke, feel the heat but you cannot find the seat of the fire.

Let me back up to the night before at Station 2 where we have our weekly training for volunteers. The goal this particular night was a 200' hose entanglement drill with a disoriented firefighter. I packed out, flipped my hood over my mask and went inside the training building. There were pallets, tires, 55 gallon barrels and other obstacles with my hose stacked on/over/under and through but no smoke or fire. The obstacle was to orient yourself and feel your way through the hose entanglement drill. The instructor made it a point to remind his students to always sound the floor making sure to always have a solid floor under you.

As I sat inside this two story burning structure 12 hours later I listened to the fire crackle in front of me with the exact same crew that I trained with the night before. Still operating in zero visibility with nozzle in hand I told my back up firefighters to prepare to advance. I hit the floor every few inches in front of me hoping that my senses would clue in on any discrepancies. My situational awareness (identify, comprehend and predict) I would say was heightened as I understand the gravity of making the wrong decision and someone else's life hanging right there with me. I continued sounding the floor, felt another door to my right, pushed it open and sounded the floor one more time. I suddenly felt a buckle of the hardwood floor planks and knew something was not right. I sounded it again and encountered the same result. I immediately told the two firefighters behind me to back out. We had encountered failure of floor integrity but I was unsure of the extent. While I am the "rookie," neither of them hesitated or questioned my decision.

After we regrouped and changed our vantage point of attack the "fire" was determined to be a slow charring fire in the wall from a lightning strike hours before the actual call. Once the smoke cleared we went back inside to check for extension and other hotspots. Visibility was greatly improved so I walked back to where I gave the orders to back out to determine what my senses had told me. The fire had burned through the wall into the flooring system there was a 6' hole in the floor only two feet away from where we stopped. The saying, "Faith in God, Trust in Training" comes to mind. Whether it was the training the night before, luck or Grace of God – remembering the basics kept us inches away from danger. I personally thanked the instructors from the night's training before so they can share this story the next time they do hose entanglement drills or fire attack drills.

This structure presented with the vent limited scenario and was just waiting for oxygen. If we would have experienced uncoordinated ventilation or barreled into the house without analyzing the situation surely conditions would have worsened very quickly and possibly a different outcome. While I am the "rookie" in this particular situation, neither of them hesitated or questioned my decision when we exited the structure. If these guys would have never seen or spoke to me before would they have still listened? This is the value of team building, training, and understanding when to follow and when to lead.

Remember the basics of your training and execute it to perfection. Anything can happen in this job, so you better be good at it. Mastery should be your new minimum standard. Drill not to get it right but until you cannot get it wrong, because the difference may only be inches away…..

In the April, 2014 edition of Fire Engineering Anthony Kastros published the article *"The American Fire Service Leadership Pandemic."* He wrote that the exceptional individuals are becoming extinct, and that many departments (and individuals in my opinion) are lacking the pass-on from these experts. Billy Goldfeder recently published the book "Pass It On" simply based on the concept of experienced leaders sharing life experiences. In order for us (as a service) to capture this "stuff" before it leaves we need to consider leadership versus followership. What does it mean and how does it apply to each situation? There will be times when you are the leader and there will be times when you need to be the follower (regardless of rank, experience, seniority), the Barn Boss understands and applies this philosophy.

Leadership versus Followership is a phrase I took out of the Crew Resource Management manual published by the International Association of Fire Chiefs. If you type in CRM for the Fire Service, you will find hundreds of articles and materials to review. In this chapter we will focus on the differences and similarities when it comes to Leaders and Followers. As everyone knows there are some vast differences such as giving and obeying orders, however, there are just as many similarities that each must have in order to be effective. Above all, no matter what side you are on today we have to be able to work together so that we stay safe, get the job done without needless injuries and deaths, and go home to our families.

Without good leaders and good followers, we seldom accomplish what we set out to do.

Crew Resource Management: Leadership and Followership

The International Association of Fire Chiefs define CRM as the effective management or use of all available resources to mitigate a situation while minimizing errors, improving safety and increasing performance. In order to obtain these goals, five factors have been identified as major components in accidents including the failure of teamwork, situational awareness, communication, decision making skills, and establishment of barriers. Each of these items is vital to the success of any fire ground, EMS, or specialty team incident. These factors must be examined, training created to emphasize, practiced before the alarm and continuously reinforced after the initial training to be effective.

Background

CRM was originally introduced in the 1970's in the aviation industry after several incidents revealed that flight crews were lacking one of the above items. One of the most tragic incidents was United Flight 173; in short, 10 people perished and 23 were injured due to the nose gear landing light bulb being burned out. The co-pilot repeatedly warned about low fuel but the pilot either did not comprehend what was happening or ignored the lesser experienced and inferior co-pilot. It has been stated that some pilots ruled with an iron fist, what they said was the bottom line, which could have been part of the problem. In the ensuing investigation it was found that the landing gear was perfectly normal and was locked in place at the time of the crash.

Do we as firefighters sometimes get fixated on the little things and miss the big picture? Sadly, the answer is yes and so did some in the aviation industry. In response, CRM training became mandatory for all flight crew and grounds crew personnel.

As CRM gained success in the aviation industry, it spread into the military, where the U.S. Navy requires annual training for all their pilots. The U.S. Naval Safety Center cited that after training two-thirds of its maintenance personnel (approximately 1200 employees) in CRM principles, they saw maintenance ground damage costs drop by 66 percent and occupational injuries decrease by 27 percent. In addition, the U.S. Coast Guard has implemented CRM training and reduced their on-the-job injuries by 74% percent.

Several other industries have developed their own CRM training including the shipping, medical, and railroad industries.

Five Factors:

Situational Awareness

The first component and arguably the most important component is situational awareness (SA). Everything on an emergency incident functions and revolves around SA, including what we base our fire ground decisions on. SA is commonly referred to as what we see or the "Big Picture." While that is part of it, it also encompasses more than just getting the "Big Picture." In Gary Klein and Caroline E. Zsambok's Naturalistic Decision Making, SA is broken down into three levels; 1) Perception of the Elements in the Environment, 2) Comprehension of the Situation and 3) Projection of Future Status. For the fire service this translates into 1) How we perceived the incident, 2) Being able to understand the incident and how the incident factors are interrelated into accomplishing our goals of the incident and 3) The use of foreseeability to predict the future factors of the incident.

Communication

What made people such as President Ronald Reagan such a success and where did the title Great Communicator come from? How did Franklin D. Roosevelt (FDR) with his unprecedented third term as president reform the nation through the Great Depression and lead the United States through World War II? The most powerful position in the world, however there is little they can do without buy-in from congress. The ability of FDR and Reagan to communicate a vision and inspire people was second to none. FDR arguably has some of the most memorable speeches, which are still as important and inspirational today, as they were when he delivered them. They also possessed the ability to listen, a commonly underestimated approach to communicating.

FDR quote:
"A day which will live in infamy..." and "The only thing to fear is fear itself..."
December 7th, 1941 in front of Congress prior to entering WWII

If situational awareness is not the most important item on the incident then communication is. Without the effective use of communication nothing seems to get accomplished and Alan Brunacini in his Expectations and Boundaries article for Fire Engineering describes this situation as a reciprocal problem. Alan Brunicini (2015) further explains that when communication fails the worker on the receiving end and the boss on the sending are both at disadvantages. "The worker suffers an effectiveness problem when not effectively connected with communication from the organization. The boss is at an even bigger disadvantage if he/she somehow gets separated from communications about the status of the work from the worker, who is the closest to our customer." The International Association of Fire Chiefs describes communication as the cornerstone of Crew Resource Management. There are six key areas to communication: sender, receiver, message, medium, filters, and feedback. It is best to use face-to-face when possible but via radio is the only option most of the time. Regardless of which method is used, the six key areas must be understood and used in order for communication to work, which in turn will assist in getting the job done.

Within these six key areas there are some other items that need to be addressed for effective communication. The first is simply being clear and concise; say what you mean and be sure to give enough detail without overloading the individual's working memory space. Here is a prime example of how even great leaders can make this same mistake (Gary Klein, Sources of Power: How People Make Decisions).

Case Study: During World War II, Winston Churchill gave the order to not engage with warships that were larger and that could destroy their individual ships. What he meant was do not try and take on ships larger than theirs and lose. Consequently, one of his admirals had surrounded an enemy warship but let it go due to the fact that it was larger and he did not want any trouble with his superiors. This was not the intent of Churchill's letter to the Admiral but without being clear and concise this is what happens. As history holds, the same enemy warship that was let go destroyed some of Britain's ships and played a large role in crippling the efforts of the British during the war. What are you saying and what are your troops hearing?

Sender – Individual sending the message. Be clear and concise without overloading the receiver.

Receiver – Individual receiving or decoding the message. Listen to the message and repeat to ensure you received the message correctly.

Message – The content of what is being delivered. In stressful situations it is important to be extremely clear, no ambiguous statements.

Medium – The channel or means of how the message is conveyed. Face to face is always the best; however, this is not always possible which means that the other parts of communication become that much more important.

Filter – The distractions involved in the station and throughout an incident can affect what is decoded by the receiver. Consider the individuals who do not know how to talk on their radio and you receive broken transmissions or just a muffled sound. Other distractions can be stress, noise, emotional, and psychological factors.

Feedback – The most important component, due to the fact that this is your check and balance on how the message was perceived. Allow the receiver to provide feedback on what they interpreted and the sender should acknowledge if it was correct or needs adjustment. This is the opportunity for others to provide information which may not have been available prior to a decision being made; however, it is prior to an action taking place.

Communicate and Listen

Do you listen to your firefighters? Do you know what is happening on all four sides and inside the structure at all times? If you do, you're better than most. The key is to allow for your followers, your firefighters, to provide you with input and information that can help you make the best possible decisions – empower them. Such as the Clarke County, Nevada incident that I mentioned earlier, the IC allowed the input of the

"Don't take it for granted that an individual will speak up when the time is there."

acting driver and it saved two crews from injuries and/or deaths. In the Fire Service, we can sometimes rule with an iron fist, our way or the highway type of attitude. Although this is sometimes needed, it's not every time. In fact, it's nearly none of the time. There are firefighters out there that have a vast amount of practical knowledge that can help you in forming your situational awareness and when it's time to make the decision. I have found that most officers believe in this type of leadership and are willing to accept it. The problem, as I mentioned earlier about being scared to sit down, much less talk my first few years, needs to be addressed with each leader and their crew. Don't take it for granted that an individual will speak up when the time is there. There are situations similar to what happened involving the USS Greenville Submarine happening every day in the field. As long as a tragic event does not occur we believe the tragedy will not happen to us. The submarine shot to the surface without using all of the proper precautions. Some of the crew knew what was going to happen when it collided with the Japanese fishing vessel killing several children, but the crew respected the captain too much to intervene. The captain had the experience, knowledge, certificates, abilities and everything else; his crew respected him too much to save him. Is that the kind of respect that you want?

Leaders must also be willing to lead by example. As a leader, never ask a firefighter or follower to do something that you, yourself, would not be willing to do or did at one point. As well, if you're going to enforce a safety policy or want your followers to act a certain way, you have to act the same way. It is not a do as I say, not as I do deal. A leader that has this mentality will never regain the credibility and respect that they have lost from acting in such a manner.

Leaders are granted authority simply because they have been given the responsibility to make the decisions that need to be made (Legitimate Power). Whether it's through the trumpets or because of their knowledge and experience, they still have the authority. In a perfect world, leaders have this authority because of their knowledge and experience, although not always the case. However, a follower must still obey their orders unless it's a safety, moral or ethical issue. As a leader though, you have two options to show your authority. You can allow the input from your followers and then decide to use their take on it or, you're still the leader, you cannot use their take on it. The other option is to discourage or worse criticize someone for thinking. There are several instances where keeping your ego in check is needed and this is one of them. Don't criticize someone for trying to develop their own mental simulation of the incident, if anything help them develop it. Most people are only trying to figure it out, they're not trying to disobey your orders. And, when stuff doesn't go your way don't blame the co-worker or employee first – many times there are outside factors. Case in point, I had an employee that was caught sleeping on shift outside of typical sleeping hours and I was asked to intervene. It would have been very easy to write him up for not following procedures however, after some discussions with him there was an underlying family factor. He was taking care of his ill mother during the day and then trying to work at night. Should this guy be punished? Or, should we figure out how to work with him? We choose to work together while understanding my expectation of what needed to occur during work hours. Years later, he is still on my team doing a great job.

Leaders have to be disciplined not to get sucked into the flame, but look at the big picture, in everything that you do. This applies to not only the fire ground but at the station as well. You must have the ability to obey the orders that are coming from above and not jumping on the bandwagon of bashing them, even if you don't agree with them. These are still policies and guidelines that you must have the discipline to follow as long as it won't get someone hurt. Always remember to keep your ego in check in times such as these, don't let the firefighters know that you disagree. If you rebel, they will eventually rebel against you. Just remember all of the stories in history about the leader being overrun.

Feedback is arguably one of the most important communication benchmarks. Remember you have to identify who it is that you are talking to, E10 B. Let them know who they need to respond back to, Command to E10 B. Develop your message in your head before you send it out. Does it make sense what you are trying to portray? Is it concise and to the point? Allow for them to provide you with feedback, just in case there are any misinterpretations or unclear tasks. If you incorporate gestures into your communication model make sure everyone knows what you are doing, tell people before hand back at the station if you have some weird gestures that you like to use. Don't get mad if they can't figure out what wave you're doing.

> I was visiting the City of Thomasville (GA) Fire Department
> and was told a story about a young individual who started in
> the dispatch center as a fire department probie many years
> ago. He was on his first night shift for the fire dispatch and
> overwhelmed with nerves trying to remember everything he
> was supposed to perform if a call came in. Well, sure enough
> a fire downtown was reported and he diligently recreated his
> training and correctly dispatched all initial resources. As the
> units started to arrive, he could hear transmission of a
> working commercial structure fire. So, now this probie is

intently listening in case he is asked to perform any other task and sure enough the first arriving battalion chief transmitted back to "Call in the Utility Department." However, that is not what the probie heard, before the end of the incident there were 40 off-duty firefighters standing in the front yard of this business. The battalion chief started asking questions to figure out what was going on and he was informed that dispatch was advised to "Call in the Whole Department." While this situation is easy to laugh at you can clearly see how important the communication model is.

Communicating with students in Northwest Fire District (Tucson, AZ) during a live fire class. Just as we brief a class, we should spend time briefing our crews before game day.

Ineffective Communication:

Command: Command to E10-B

E10:   E10 to Command

Command:	E10 I need you to come out here and pull an additional 1 ¾" to the front door. I also want you to grab an additional tool to check for extension on the second floor. While you're at it make sure that you're sounding the floor below you and don't let the fire get behind you.
E10:	E10 to….. and you get run over by someone else…
Command:	Command to E14 report to staging…

As you can see, Command made his report to long and the firefighter will probably forget something that Command said. However, a lot of what he said should be practiced at the station before the call and if he truly has to say the types of things such as which hose line to pull. If so, there are more issues than just communication. Command did not let E10 provide any feedback and now we do not know if the message was understood. Feedback is essential and the same applies at the day to day operations inside the station. Let's look at effective communication.

Effective Communication:

Command:	Command to E10-B
E10:	E10 to Command
Command:	E10 take a second line, 2nd floor, fire attack and check for extension.
E10:	E10 is clear on additional line, 2nd floor, fire attack and checking for extension.

Command: Correct E10

As you can see this time it was much easier and directly to the point. The feedback was allowed and Command acknowledged E10 understood what Command needed accomplished. It is vital that information pass in this form and face to face is even better if it's applicable. The value in the short and concise message comes when someone else is trying to pass along important information that needs to be heard and acted upon immediately, such as a safety hazard, mayday, or imminent collapse situation.

In fact, you want to be as clear and concise as E19's conversation which I may or may not have been involved in. In the cab of an old Sutphen with the windows down, the engine revving in the center of the cab, returning to quarters from an incident – clear. Somehow one of the portable radio transmission buttons had being pressed and through all of these distractions and noise, Battalion Chief Wilbur Holt was sitting at Station 19 upon our return to discuss the non-politically correct underlying tones of the movie Wizard of Oz. The message was so distinct and clear he automatically knew what station to go to, at the same time everyone on duty is calling our cells phone – unfortunately none of us answered our cell phones.

Decision Making

As we discussed earlier, situational awareness (SA) is vital to how we make decisions. One study that I recently read examining military fighter pilots showed that their decisions were directly based on how they perceived the situation. They may have made the right call for their perception of the incident but they did not perceive the situation correctly, so they failed. In essence, having a strong background in SA can help us make the needed decisions within our limited scope of time. In conjunction with SA, we need good communication relayed back to the individual making the decisions. The decision maker is now capable of establishing their strategies and tactics for the incident. As well, they can compare what they are being relayed from their firefighters to what they see on the outside. Once this has occurred, the leader can make a sound decision that will have a positive outcome on the incident.

Recent studies in the field of Naturalistic Decision Making, which is based on making decisions in a natural setting (real life environment) have brought forward several considerations for training. This training is to be designed around Mental Simulation, Pattern Matching, Story Building and the Power of Intuition. Each of these areas plays a part in how we relate what is in front of us to our brain and then we make a decision based on our knowledge and experience. Nothing can replace on-scene experience but that is not always something that we can control, with this study we have found the need for more training. Using scenario based or tactical decision games is a great way for a firefighter to begin to build patterns and stories of how to operate at an incident, without actually being on scene to learn. Mental Simulation and Intuition will only come once we show a complete understanding of how one factor relates to the next even when it is not directly in front of us.

Teamwork

How often do we actually train on performing as a team? How often do we actually examine what we do as a team that makes us function effectively or fail effectively? As firefighters we train constantly to function as part of a team, however do we always carry that to the field? When a team has worked together and has bonded, they seem to function as the right hand knows without saying what the left hand is doing which is implicit communication. A fire brother of mine, David Bullard, provided me with the analogy that the "crew that eats ice cream together, talks less at fires." His point is that building a relationship with your crew encompasses learning each other's weaknesses and strengths, which translates into a high degree of implicit communication. In addition, one major aspect of teamwork is understanding how to talk to an individual when offering a suggestion or concern. Having and showing mutual respect for all members on the team is essential to the team excelling and practicing leadership-followership techniques.

A leader must understand that every team will go through stages of team building. These stages will not always look the same depending on various factors however; we all know what a good team looks like. Bruce Tuckman named these stages forming, storming, norming, and performing – in the order they occur. The leader should understand that this process occurs with every team and prepare for it. We will all disagree at some point. However, if we trust each other, believe in our experiences, and our point of reference is accurate we will respect our peers and be more open to change and feedback. These team building drills, along with experience together, will display strengths and weaknesses. The value in this is that we can now optimize the strengths of each person and be aware of the weaknesses of each person.

While all of my special operations team can perform every task required during a high angle situation. There are a few who excel at rigging, a few at packaging, and a few at commanding the incident. One of my exercises for developing the skills of each individual while allowing each individual to display their skill set competencies is the simple competition. I set the group up in two different formats, the first is a one on one competition and the second is a two on two competition. It doesn't matter what the actual drill is but we will use a simple Z-Rig with a change of direction set up. I allow the individuals to discover the value of teamwork for themselves without anyone else having to teach it. Both groups want to win and I want them to be successful, so I allow them to stage all of the parts they will need and prepare their strategy for deployment. Their desire to win the head-to-head competition allows the individual to be open to how others are performing the task. They are open to new ideas, willing to accept critiques and not afraid of change. If another method is more efficient, the individual will adapt. All of these items are brought together through team work.

Although, above I called the Z-Rig a simple task it requires a

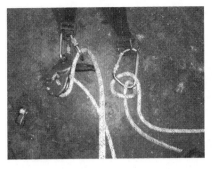

series of steps which some can be performed simultaneously, others must be performed sequentially. For example, one member must establish the anchor, while the other deploys the actual rope in a Z pattern and determine where the pulleys and Kong Duck (rope grab) must be placed. One of the transition points is where the rope deployment and anchor must be combined through the use of gear with the Petzl I'D, picture to the left (tool which grabs the rope and keeps from descending but allows members to pull through the tool when ascending). If the rope is not established properly or if the anchor man does not pay attention to the direction of the rope (which side is the load side) the system will not work at all. The last transition is demonstrating the raising and lowering of the rescuer. All of these components are valuable and not one of them can be shortcut, left out, or improperly applied. In addition to deploying the system, there are several safety factors which have to be recognized and thought through making this a stressful situation.

However, at the end of the competition everyone starts to learn each other's skills and learns how to improve their abilities. We typically will perform these competitions 10 – 15 times in a row; however, you may only work with the same person twice. This approach forces you to communicate and adapt based on your partner. This approach can be used in many different formats and does not have to be used just as a rope competition. Other examples would be deploying various hose loads, staging primary searches in fire station, deploying standpipe operations, VEIS operations with a training tower. Read the Stranded Island Exercise at the end of chapter as one way to build teamwork and it can be used as an Ice Breaker.

Forming – This is the initial stage of the team developing and typically everyone is looking for guidance from the leader. Team members begin to develop perceptions concerning work ethics, values, knowledge and skill sets, and personalities. I find it important to perform team building skills early on to assist in breaking the ice but also to attempt to identify the strengths of each member in a non-threatening or stressful situation. I believe it is also important to establish a relationship as leader and follower through one or a combination of the leadership styles we discuss in this book. Establishing the expectations also sets the tone for where the bar will be set and (hopefully) inspires and motivates your peers to strive for greatness.

Storming – This is the second stage of team building and typically is the stage where team members begin to open up and voice opinions. This is also the stage where inner groups within the team may start to develop due to common ideas and thoughts grouping together. The most important item for the leader here is to relate everything to the vision of the group, however, allow people to challenge respectively. Look for the value in creative and innovative challenges. Is there a better way to do it?

There may be times where Type A personalities begin to voice strong opinions and the one feeling we have gets hurt so we rebuttal – as a leader you may have to sit the group down together and readdress the vision of what we are here to accomplish and what milestones we have met. This is also a time where I discuss the dynamics of team building. The last group that had this situation with a bunch of Type A personalities I told them, "this is what I wanted you to do, we are making progress finally, I was waiting for you to start expressing your feelings." Then, I explained the Forming, Storming, Norming, Performing process and, for the most part, they all become enlightened and start the norming process. The key as you transition into the norming stage is to continue to informally revisit the vision with each team member. Legendary, Retired Phoenix Fire Chief Alan Brunacini refers to this as Organizational Alignment. This keeps us aligned and builds the relationship between leader and follower.

Norming – This is the third stage and is where team members start to work together and build off of each other's strengths. This is where the team becomes more important than the "I" and you see compromising begin to occur. In extreme cases, I have actually seen a firefighter give up the nozzle for someone who does not always get the chance – rare but I have seen it. This is also the stage where team members constantly joke with each other and if you are not part of the team you will not understand it. As a piece of advice in the fire station, if people stop openly joking with you, you are not in the norming stage and you are being alienated from the group. During this stage, trust has been developed and team members understand and respect the input of each other.

Performing – This is the last and forth stage of the team building process. During this stage team members perform at their highest level and conflict is non-existent. While there may be challenges, team members are quick to understand the best practice and work through any differences. Team members will build each other up and protect each other because the team is above all. Major accomplishments and milestones begin to be met and experiences are developed which can be tied to future endeavors. As the team begins to work through incident after incident they develop more and more experiences to build off of. Once the team reaches this stage they feed off of each other and their motivation to succeed can't be beat. Shriberg and Shriberg describe high performing team characteristics as understanding their individual jobs, how their job affects the team and how their role is related to the bigger picture and will serve as a component of accomplishing the team's shared goal. In the fire service, one common acronym which has a couple of different variations FTM:PTB represents this stage. The International Fraternal Order Of Leatherheads Society calls this For The Men: Protect The Brothers.

Characteristics of High Performing Teams as outlined by George Manning and Kent Curtis, authors of The Art of Leadership:

1. Clear Goals
2. Results-Driven
3. Competent Team Members
4. A Shared Commitment
5. Collaboration
6. Standards of Excellence
7. External Support and Recognition
8. Principled Leadership

Stranded on an Island Exercise

Directions: Split the team into groups and give them 5 minutes to select a leader. Once a leader is selected, take them to a different area and explain to them your group crash landed on an unknown island in the Pacific Ocean. Nobody is hurt, however, the plane is not intact but you do have all parts of the plane. The group can ask for three items to appear on the island but they can only use skills/equipment for which they have experience with (for example: you cannot ask for a plane if you have never flown a plane). The group must also decide if they wish to stay on the island or attempt to get off the island. There is no right or wrong answer; however, it starts to make people think about how valuable diversity of each individual can be. It also demonstrates certain characteristics of how we choose leaders or how they choose themselves and others follow. As well, review with the groups the different types of leaders and followers. This exercise also gets at the importance of communication and the ability to relay directions from person to person. Look for the situation of messages being misinterpreted.

Barriers or "Safety Nets"

Barriers or "Safety Nets" are put in place so that as humans when we make a mistake there is something there to catch us. No matter who we are, how much training or education, how much experience or how many awards we have achieved we are at some point going to make a mistake. The key is to understand our weaknesses and to never repeat the same mistake. Barriers can come in many different forms. Some of the obvious ones are SOP's/SOG's, effective training, and core competency books. There are others that will increase your budget slightly but are extremely beneficial such as updated equipment and increased technology.

There are many other items that can be incorporated into a barrier, some may require a little more work than others but items such as Incident Safety Officers established on all scenes, RIC teams established with proper resources and staffing, acting and company officer training, and drivers training programs are a few.

One other area that can be of great benefit is the use of checklist and worksheets to help the officer's on-scene; this includes the Incident Commander, Safety Officer, Rehab Group Supervisor, and RIC Group Team Leader. These can help remind the officers of the tasks to be completed, benchmarks, safety concerns and crew locations. However, with all great things there are downfalls. We still have not found a way to checklist or talk a fire out. It is important to remember that the checklist is only as effective as the expertise of the individual using it. We must still train and educate the same as before and still allow the officer the discretion to change the plan or the order of the checklist as they see fit.

Applications

Applications are the most important aspect of training and help us figure out all the intricate parts of an operation. When we can actually build a story in our head by performing a task or operation we will be more apt to retain and recall the story than by traditional means of just reading about or seeing an operation performed. There are activities that can be performed in the station or developed by training staff to incorporate CRM components into the training session. The two examples below are low cost and can be conducted mostly with items already in the station.

Medical Training

Allow your officer's to perform a mock cardiac arrest in the station. The company should be notified in advance and take the apparatus out of service for about 30 minutes. The firefighters and paramedics will start in their apparatus as if they just pulled up at the incident and then the time starts. They jump off the apparatus, grab their equipment, and start working. There is some stress added with this being a timed event just as we are timed in the field. As the team performs the scenario some things just flow while others have to be communicated. Items such as starting IV's, obtaining vitals, and ensuring all of the equipment is operationally ready are signs of a team that has performed together before. This allows the lead paramedic to worry about the more important items. After the scenario, the officer critiques the crew on what they did well and where they could improve.

Fire Training

Another easy opportunity for training with CRM involves conducting scenario based fire training. Throw out a problem, single family dwelling with fire on Side A, put a picture up on the screen or wall and let the firefighter handle the incident. Scenario based training is some of the best training that firefighters can receive without actually being involved with the real life experience part of it. If the firefighter leading the training wishes to add a sense of stress to the scenario, start timing the incident to force decisions to be made and have the other crew members participate as responding apparatus. Constructive criticism should be provided in a formal manner as well.

Leadership

There have been various theories of leadership developed over the years from born leaders to developed leaders, Situational Leadership, Servant Based, Path-Goal Theory, Leader-Member Exchange, etc... While I believe that it is important to review, study and understand the different thought processes concerning leadership, anyone that has been in a leadership position (and been effective) will tell you that you are slowing your growth as a leader if you attempt to pigeon hole yourself into one style of leadership. For example, how many people want a leader who practices equality based leadership, in other words everyone is treated equal. At first glance this may seem wise; however, this practice will not positively affect everyone the same and will negatively impact key players, possibly. The situation that comes to mind surrounds two employees, one is above average and always arrives early for work while the other is clocking in a minute before shift change and is average at best. Following an aggressive attendance policy, if either of these individuals are tardy they should both be disciplined the same regardless of their performance. Both of these incidents occurred over time with two distinctive outcomes. The first individual who exhibited above average performance and was always early was not formally disciplined however; we had a discussion concerning the situation and agreed upon expectations. This benefit of a doubt provided this employee was motivation for this employee because they saw it as trust and faith in them from their direct leadership. The second employee who was at best average on performance and arriving a minute before shift change was formally disciplined. This employee also was motivated after our discussion and saw it as a chance to improve. Following the equality theory would not have allowed these outcomes to occur and would have possibly been devastating to both employees performance.

Command and Control Leadership

Around 1916, Henri Fayol from France developed an administrative and management style of leadership based on 5 components: planning, organizing, commanding, coordinating and controlling. He believed that Commanding and Controlling were essential in a clear command structure. As you review his list of the 14 Principles consider how many of these principles are ingrained (or have been) in the public service as a top down approach to managing people? The part for you, as your own leader, is to determine which apply for which situation.

1. Specialization (Division of Labor)
2. Authority with Responsibility

3. Discipline

4. Unity of command

5. Unity of direction

6. Subordination of individual interests

7. Remuneration

8. Centralization

9. Chain of Command

10. Order

11. Equity

12. Lifetime jobs (for good workers)

13. Initiative

14. Esprit de corps

Servant Based Leadership

"I stand here before you not as a prophet but as a humble servant of you, the people. Your tireless and heroic sacrifices have made it possible for me to be here today. I therefore place the remaining years of my life in your hands."

These are the words of Nelson Mandela on February 11th, 1990 after being freed from prison after 27 years in South Africa.

Before there was Servant Based Leadership which was coined in the 1970s by Robert Greenleaf in his "Leader as Servant" publication, there was the Hawthorne Effect. A series of experiments from 1927 – 1932, at the Hawthorne Plant of the Western Electric Company in Cicero, Illinois. Elton Mayo notated that if you provide attention to your employees and their needs, you will typically see an increase in their performance. In essence, if you take care of your employees and provide for them, they will return the efforts. Recall the earlier examples of the sports drinks and challenge coin presentation. These are small examples of motivation but also internal self-worth and is an example of the employee seeing that the leader cares.

Fast-forward 40 years, the Servant Based Leadership Theory states that the leader is there for the employees. This leader empowers by creating opportunities (discussed earlier in the article on mentoring with David Rhodes), develops intuition and the ability to expect the unexpected (Gary Klein's research and the Fire Engineering Article Expect the Unexpected) and listens to the needs of their employees and of those that they are mentoring. One of the items that I have found throughout my career is that the higher rank and responsibilities I achieved the harder I worked for those below me. Your employees will and can make or break you, they are your most valuable resource and asset. Another perspective of this style is that you develop initiative in your employees for them to go out and lead in their own rights'. This becomes an organization of leaders versus a leader and many followers – this is one component of developing Barn Bosses. There is no greater pride than developing people in your organization and seeing them promoted to various ranks within the organization.

"Surround yourself with talent and you will be considered a talented man, failure to properly motivate your employees could be the cause for losing everything."

Situational Leadership

The Situational Leadership Theory supports what we discussed early concerning there not being one all-knowing leadership style which can be applied to all situations. However, Kenneth Blanchard and Paul Hersey presented the perspective that each situation is different depending on numerous variables. They suggest using one of four actions to lead an individual based on the competence of the task at hand, social and emotional commitment to the task and the exhibited readiness of the individual to lead. The four actions suggested are directing, coaching, supporting and delegating.

For example:

You may direct the application of a new tactic if you have an inexperienced crew. Yet, you may decide to provide coaching points based on experiences and knowledge to a competent crew for an extrication exercise. If the competence of the operating crew works at a very high level you may elect to simply provide support such a providing resources while observing from a high level overview. Lastly, for your most competent individuals and crews you simply delegate the task and generally consider it complete. If your battalion chief delegates to you the task of riding-up as the acting officer they are suggesting they have competence in your skills and abilities in many cases.

Now, how do we achieve these various levels of trust between crews and leaders? We train in various situations and allow the up-and-comers to experience similar experiences in environments that are realistic yet provide for mistakes to be made. Some of the greatest learning situation I have been involved in occurred when I failed. After you provide these opportunities through training ensure that you critique the training, however do not provide all of the answers during the training scenario. We must learn to interpret our own situations based on our knowledge and skills – if a mistake is made performing this in a training situation, this is when we want this to occur. Gary Klein suggest in "Streetlights and Shadows" that concurrent feedback during the training will increase performance during the training evolution but it can set the trainee up for failure during a real incident because they were never given a chance to interpret the situation on their own.

Bringing It All Together

Leaders have to be able to communicate effectively, lead by example, exhibit authority, be disciplined, keep your ego in check, listen to the firefighters, provide clear paths for task completion and a host of many more traits. However, one of the most important tasks is the ability to communicate with each other, with as minimum amount words as possible. On the fire ground, nobody has time to write directions or draw a map for anyone. The task needs to be completed now, not 10 minutes from now. How do we get to that point of execution? This is what we call implicit communication, this is when we have worked together, trained together, we know each other's weaknesses and strengths, and we know how to work with each other. Experience with each individual is a big factor in this, but so is training. Training is where we learn about each other long before we run the call and then try to figure out each other. Structured, hands-on training, even if it's simply putting your gear on and performing a search in the station. This will allow us to learn each other's habits and tendencies. Some of these habits and tendencies will need to be corrected but some we can adapt to, or it may be establishing options that we can use at future incidents. As a leader, you should be able to get a good feeling for what you can expect to be accomplished at this point by your followers.

Followership

Just as well, followers have a great deal of responsibility on them in this game of leaders and followers. Followers must also keep their ego out of it, be disciplined, practice communication and have the ability to listen to their leaders. In addition, followers have the responsibility of always being on their "A Game," be respectful, and be flexible to changing conditions.

If as a follower you wish to provide input, you have the obligation to make sure that you know what you are talking about and bring up valid points and concerns. You don't need to talk just for your own health. This requires the follower to constantly train, and to constantly work with their crew. Most of the time in order to achieve this level, it requires the firefighter to do some work or training when others are not. It is up to each individual to build your own knowledge and skills bank. The great thing about it is that once you learn and master them, you get to pass them on to the other firefighters. This will ultimately make your company and crew that much better.

As a follower, you should study the communication phrase that we laid out for the leaders. You should also study the way in which you provide information to an officer. Earlier we talked about tact and the ability to use it. This is extremely useful when addressing a commanding officer in any situation. Remember to always be respectful and address them by their proper title. Tell them what your concern is and what might be an option. Hell, make them think they came up with it if it's the right thing to do. No one should care who gets the credit as long as it was done right and no one got hurt. Then, the kicker, ask what they think about the new idea? What would be their concern for addressing the situation from your point-of-view? So, it should go something like this:

Who:	Lt. Johnson
What:	Is there any concerns with the tilt slab wall when the roof is falling?
Solution:	I was just thinking, the instructor said something about it in the class that you sent me to. Should we back up any?
Kicker:	Yeah, let's back up a few feet.

It can be as simple as this. Who are you talking to, what is your concern, what's a solution, and the kicker?

Being respectful will bring you much respect yourself, even if you weren't respected in the manner that you should have been. Just remember their day will come, you may just be their boss one day, just take it with a grain of salt. This is one of the hardest parts in practice even if the leader doesn't know or understand the situation the way you perceive the situation, it's still not a reason to argue or fight, especially on-scene. There was a recent case in the news where a firefighter punched a captain in the face on-scene and that firefighter was not only fired, but escaped jail time by giving up his right to ever work for another fire department. There is nothing that can't be handled back at the station and after a cool down period. Make it a practice to handle everything in-house, if possible. It is never a good idea to air dirty laundry, unless there is some career ending event such as a law requiring you too.

Motivators

Maslow in Firefighter Terms

Pull out your old Instructor I manuals or maybe you saw it in a past leadership class; however, wherever you found it start reviewing Maslow's Hierarchy of Needs. While there are different variations since he published this in 1964, the basis remains the same. As a Barn Boss, it's not your job to memorize them – that means nothing, however you should understand the basics of what makes people tick. If people are hungry (physiological needs – first rung), they are not going to listen to anything you say because their basic needs have not been satisfied. Some of you may laugh at the importance but for those of you who have been in this situation understand it completely. As the list ascends from the ground level up: Physiological Needs (food, shelter, safety), Safety Needs (safe at work, job security), Belongingness Needs (work group), Self-Esteem Needs (status, recognition), and Self-Actualization Needs (growth, creativity). In firefighter terms, we need sleep and food (physiological); don't threaten with job security/let me use good equipment (Safety Needs); teamwork (Belongingness); promote your crew when they perform well (Self-Esteem Needs); and create opportunities/mentor (Self-Actualization Needs).

Reinforcement Theory

The Reinforcement Theory looks at positively and negatively using enforcers to create either a favorable condition or an unfavorable condition. When someone performs well and you want to show your appreciation you perform some action to display this appreciation. A few years back, members of the City of Gray Volunteer Fire Department and Jones County Fire Rescue responded to an apartment fire with an elderly lady entrapped. Upon arrival several of the members came together to size up the situation, made entry, performed the search and successfully extricated the lady. This is obviously a stressful task with many emotions which very few firefighters actually get to take part in and the victim survive for any length of time. The reinforcement came in many forms from the appreciation of the family, the admiration of fellow members, and formal recognition at the state capital during firefighter appreciation week.

On the flip side, when someone performs an action that you wish to deter them from repeating you deploy a different approach, however, it is still used as a re-enforcer. If someone is late for shift change you may decide to formally document the situation. However, if you are critiquing an incident and would prefer that a different tactic be used you may decide to coach the firefighter by understanding what they saw and then you assist them in how you would have interpreted the incident. The point is that there are various methods for reinforcing the behaviors you wish to repeat or not repeat.

Expectancy Theory

Victor Vroom developed the expectancy theory in 1964 which states that if you understand the expectations of those surrounding you, you can use this information to influence and motivate their behavior. Vroom stated that there are three components which effect motivation: Expectancy, Instrumentality, and Valence.

Expectancy is defined as the perception of an individual (remember, perception is reality) that effort will improve performance.

Instrumentality is defined as the perception of an individual where specific outcomes are linked to their performance.

Valence is defined as the individual's perception of the worth of the outcome.

For example, Saturday and Sunday are training days and there are chores to be completed. However, this becomes an interference with college and pro football, at least during the fall. If you find yourself in a similar situation, frame up the training and chores in this manner. "Crew – games start at 12:30 PM and fully expect to be watching football in between running calls, however, we have jobs that must be accomplished first. Let's hit the chores and then run through our drills. I expect full involvement and I expect the drills to be completed to a competent level." If your crew finds value in watching the home team on the weekends (valence), you have linked effort of the firefighters to the value of football (instrumentality) and you have set the standard for the amount of effort required to reach a competent level (expectancy) you have a successful outcome. While this may seem small, sometimes it is the small things that matter most, and it may be the small things that people remember the most when they have to exert even greater efforts later on.

When considering how to motivate people you must first learn to communicate with them. Listen to what they value and what their needs are. Remember that every individual is different just as every generation is different. However, even with understanding the generations be careful not to stereotype because even people within the same generation are different. Once you determine what is valued amongst your crew members begin to link efforts and performance to the outcomes which are valued.

"Learn what your troops value, link their effort and performance to that value."

Key Points

- Leaders and followers should use clear and concise communication.

- Practice implicit communication and plan for it.

- Leaders should lead by example, have authority, discipline, keep your ego in check, listen to the firefighters, and provide clear paths for task completion.

- Followers should keep their ego out of it, be disciplined, have the ability to listen to their leaders, be respectful, and flexible.

Chapter 8

"Anyone can hold the helm when the sea is calm."

Publilius Syrus

Adversity: Having Tough Skin

Adversity is a natural fear for all people and no one wishes to be a part of adversity. However, adversity is kind of like growing up, it's just going to happen sooner or later. The key for any individual that steps out in front is to learn to deal with the adversity and learn to decipher between constructive criticism and negativity. This negative stress is referred to as distress or the unhealthy type. Handling adversity is becoming a lost art in today's society between everything offending people, people never being told no and everyone gets a trophy. Pittsburg Steelers Linebacker James Harrison's decision to give back his children's participation trophies was widely publicized. His stance was that his children did not earn a real trophy and he believed you work hard to earn everything. This comes from a no scholarship walk-on from Kent State who played his first season in Europe and was cut from the Baltimore Ravens. He could have easily given up, however, we would have never known the 5 time Pro Bowl, 2 time Super Bowl Champion and 2008 NFL Defensive Player of the Year, synonymous with Steelers defense. James Harrison, learned to overcome adversity and each challenge made him stronger.

Learning to deal with adversity will show your level of professionalism, help you gain experience and respect. Challenges are necessary for identity, growth, health and real happiness. And risk is essential for a challenge (Marono, 2008). The age old saying of what doesn't kill you only makes you stronger, really is true and can be applied in multiple situations.

The adversity that we face throughout life becomes a credit and guide for where and what we face today. We learn what actions work and what actions don't work either through our direct experiences or through watching our leaders and mentors. This stress (adversity) actually can be a motivator and encourage us to reach beyond our current level of satisfaction in life.

Our brains are not wired to settle for status quo, however, without exercise they will become weak and fragile. New inputs such as new information, experiences, and environments all play a part in developing our brain and releasing brain growth factors such as dendrites and synapses. If we don't introduce some levels of healthy stress upon ourselves our minds will lose all dexterity. This is very similar to if you don't drill with your gloves on – you lose the touch of dexterity when attempting a task.

Former City of Atlanta Fire Chief Kelvin Cochran discusses adversity in his Developing Authentic Leadership Presentation, which describes exactly what I am talking about. He talks about growing up and the challenges that he faced in the process of developing into his dream job as a firefighter. The challenges that he faced growing up developed him into the leader that he is today and gives him a sense of appreciation for the amount of work that it takes to accomplish a goal. If everything was always given to us, how would we learn to accept failure? How would we know what it means to work for a greater good? Or, simply, what do we do in hard times, just give up or do we learn to dig down deep? The answer to all of these is that we must learn to face adversity head on, whether it's on the job or in our personal life and it adds to our experience bank.

Any individual that steps out in front of a group or puts themselves in a vulnerable position is bound to face some adversity. One of my most memorable events from early in my career concerning adversity on a professional level occurred the same time I was selected to serve as a training officer with GCFES. Comments from select field personnel were made to individuals that I worked with, however never directly to me, concerning me being too young and inexperienced. Maybe they were right; however I accepted the challenge of that position and intended to do my best at it. According to my officers, I performed at a high enough level in the field and that impressed someone in a higher position which gave me this opportunity; continue to carry yourself in the same manner. Just as well, keep everything in perspective, if this individual could do a better job, they could have put in for the position the same as I did.

The comment bothered me at first but ultimately drove me to be the best at what I do. Over time, after a day or week of blowing off steam, I learned to turn these comments into constructive criticism and honestly look into what they are saying. I would ask myself, "Is there any validity to what they are saying, even if it seems exaggerated, is there a way for me to improve based upon their comments?" My thoughts are that if I could win over an individual that didn't originally approve of my position then I was probably doing what I needed to do. This is much easier said than done and it's a never ending process. In addition, it is a credit to your work ethic and a huge accomplishment when you are able to do this. It is very much like controlling the air conditioning in the classroom, you cannot please everyone; however, you still strive to make it the best possible environment for everyone.

There has been another situation where the Reply All button was used and a chief officer in a different department typed a few words that may have been out of line for the situation and caused others to join in. Where there is blood, there are sharks….. As the vice-chair of this organization I could have responded very quickly and made myself feel better, but ultimately that decision would have hurt my credibility or I could wait and talk to a mentor before responding. Over the next hour, I typed 100 email responses but chose not to send any emails or phone calls on the advice of a mentor. This is where I learned to never directly reply in an email. If it was truly important they would have called so time is not a factor. A couple of items to consider with email: 1) you are always braver in email than face-to-face which can be a very negative approach, 2) you lose the face-to-face interpretation and contact that is very valuable in these situations.

Before the day was out, what was biting at me in an extreme way turned out to be just fine and this chief officer not only called to apologize but publicly apologized. The respect I gained from leaders in other departments was a big boast to my local credibility. Lesson here is to never hit reply all, don't respond to emails immediately, and keep your cool. It will all work out. To this day, this particular chief and I are still friends. I have found that when there are issues, cooler heads will prevail, and time is a friend in most cases. There is also a magical development of solutions when you can discuss via phone or (best case) sit down face-to-face and work through the issues.

As well, a majority of the time individuals that criticize don't understand what you are trying to accomplish. Two items generally come into play here, un-informed or predetermined mis-conception. In Georgia, we have the Georgia Smoke Divers Program; it's a physically and mentally intensive program. The bottom line is that if you don't adequately prepare, you won't make it. From the un-informed, I received very weird facial expressions and comments from individuals when I would work out in gear in front of my downtown volunteer station on my off days. I guess it's an awkward event to see a firefighter doing lunges down the street while breathing air. To their defense they had no clue what I was training for, the best thing to do here is to just laugh it off. Even though it was ultimately going to benefit the citizens and my department from the knowledge and skills I brought back, they would never be able to understand.

For the predetermined mis-conception, firefighters on the career side had heard about the program but had not investigated for themselves and accepted whatever rumor they heard. I heard everything from it's nothing but for your pride and ego to all you do is run in gear all day with no objective. It's important that you do your own investigation and determine what is for you. We can't allow these types of comments to influence our behaviors or we will never move forward, it would be easy to give in, but what do you gain from giving in? This program pushed me to perform skillfully at limits that I have never encountered before. It comes down to being another tool on the fire ground for me to rely on, however adversity came with it before I even made it to the adversity of the course itself.

As anyone can see, there are numerous types of adversity: internal and external that we have to learn to manage. Learning to manage adversity will help us develop our own authentic leadership style. The experiences that we face today may be the situation that we are asked to handle tomorrow. These experiences will assist you in becoming a better individual and leader. The key to managing these adversities is learning to take a negative and make it a positive. For example, maybe you have heard of some of these individuals and there adversities:

Albert Einstein – Parents and teachers believed he was below average and did not speak a word until the age of 3. His parents wished for him to be an electrical engineer however he failed the entrance exam. The whole theoretical physics stuff was something he worked on in his spare time.

George Washington – First United States of America President and war hero could not spell and had poor grammar.

JJ Watts – Did not receive a scholarship to play football at the college level. He was a walk-on at the University of Wisconsin.

Several of these situations have presented themselves over my years as a leader. Specifically, as an officer, individuals want to know how to deal with different situations in the station and the classroom. This includes everything from the extremely smart individual to the disruptive student, which all can include some form of adversity. Turning your adverse experiences into a positive outcome creates a level of credibility within your program. As I learned to handle the different personalities in the classroom it made me better at handling the personalities at the station. As a training officer, I saw and managed hundreds of personalities from different backgrounds every week, requiring me to adapt to a changing environment frequently. These situations provided me with tons of experience to apply back in the field.

One of the other positive outcomes of adversity is allowing it to keep you humble. Always remember where you came from and that you are never above the people that you work with now or in the past. Being humble is extremely important to becoming a successful leader, regardless if it's leading a crew or a department. Allowing a certain amount of adversity and firehouse joking to occur, more than likely shows that your comrades want to relate with you, they want to be a part of what is going on. My department has the saying that if they're not joking with you/at you, then they probably don't like you. However, there is a fine line between harassment and having fun, if it does not break any rules then what is the harm with it. Learn to accept firehouse joking, no matter where you go or what you do, have tough skin and don't wear your feelings on your sleeves. Have fun with it, tell something on yourself.

When I was a rookie, about three months on the job at Station 15 in downtown Lawrenceville I received a phone call about 0710 one week day morning that startled me. What startled me was the voice on the other end "This is Lou, where are you?" As you all know the cluster effect going on inside your head in that first 60 seconds after waking –that cluster was occurring at this very moment. Attempting to comprehend what is going on and then trying to conjure up some explanation was just too much. All I could think was "oh *&%@." I managed not to say "oh *&%@" to lieutenant but that I was on my way (I failed to tell him I was still asleep). I had successfully made it through recruit school without being late once but now that I'm in the field I found myself late for work. I was not just 5 or 10 minutes, I was still asleep late – 40 minutes late. I remember driving down Highway 316, which is about like an interstate, heart pounding, scared that I had lost my job, driving 90 miles per hour.

I eventually pulled into the station about 40 minutes later and I will never forget the scolding I received. This particular scolding did not come from the captain or lieutenant, it came from someone I did not even know on an opposite shift. Normally, most people do not mind holding over for valid reasons, as they are paid overtime, however this was not my lucky day. When I walked into the station to set up my gear up on Truck 15, the senior firefighter I was relieving ripped into me ensuring to cover every derogatory term there is in the dictionary for being late and anything that describes being late. He proceeded to provide advice on how immature and disrespectful I was for the chain of events which made him hold over. By the time the captain got to me there was not much more he could do that had not already been done.

While I probably did not deserve the lashing I received, it did reinstate the commitment and focus that I needed to have in order to fulfill my duties. This event also taught me to pay attention to details, be punctual, prepare for the unforeseen and never be late again. So, to this day I have two alarm clocks and I have not been late since. I thought that after the first event the storm would pass and I would be allowed to quietly be forgiven for my tardiness and that someone else would screw up and forget about my mistake. However, this would not happen either as I was reminded everyday by Driver/Engineer Gary Wirl. For my remaining time at Station 15, I carried the nick name Timex. You can get mad about it and receive further punishment, or admit your mistake and move on.

Every individual will face adversity in some form or fashion. The key is learning to decipher between what is important and unimportant in life. Learn to take the negative situations and turn them into positive outcomes, share your experiences and provide information on what worked and what did not work for you. As a leader, during an adverse time, remember this – "Leadership is solving problems. The day soldiers stop bringing you their problems, is the day you have stopped leading them. They have either lost confidence that you can help them or concluded you do not care. Either case is a failure of leadership" (Retired General Colin Powell). Through this we have simply turned it into lessons learned and training experiences. Learning to manage these situations will build your credibility, and build your character as an individual and a leader. If nothing else is taken away from this discussion, take this: Never let someone else's negative comments and actions decide for you what you are going to do. Stay true to yourself, who and what you want to be and do. As the Smoke Divers Creed goes…. *"I will not hear those who weep and complain, for their disease is contagious."*

Never settle for just getting by but don't be afraid to step up to the plate if you see something that needs to be handled. However, when you decide to step up, do it with the utmost respect and tact, show that what you are doing is from your heart and is about what you stand for. Be the catalyst in your department that is a constant motivator and creator of training and safety practices, and live the gospel as you preach it. Have the tough skin and don't be afraid.

Here are a few of my failures:

I have thought back over my career and counted some of my numerous failures, which is humbling to say the least, but from every failure there is something to learn. There is a chance to improve the skill, knowledge, or effort. For those attempting to move up in their career or accomplish some astonishing feat, the one piece of advice I can offer is to not give up. So, humble yourself and then analyze what could have been better. Please don't laugh too hard......

High School Failure

I did not want to get started to late in life at failing, so I started in high school. I was your typical working, sports loving, top of the class C student. I was even told at one point that if I didn't know what I wanted to do by then (by an English teacher), I would probably be a failure in life. Great Advice! Knowing now what I don't wish I knew then (too much stress to enjoy trying to grow up) I realize now I could have applied myself more. I remember bringing home an A in Government one year (yes, once) and my pops, thinking he would be thrilled, he replied "what happened to the rest of the classes?" Go figure.... Eventually, once I found my interest I made the Dean's list once or twice during my bachelor's degree and now finishing my Masters now with a 4.0. I guess there is still time

15 years later to make something of myself. And, for the English teacher (who may have had a valid point) the Training Officer's Desk Reference was published last year by Jones and Bartlett and you are reading the second book.

Can't Teach a Dead Horse to Die

After several years on the line as a firefighter in Metro Atlanta, I decided it was time to take the dive into instructing at the department fire academy, which became the door to everything I've accomplished. What's the worst that could happen? Up to this point I had put together some training at the station and really attempted to learn as much as I could possibly take in. I started at the academy teaching under another instructor with the recruit program and eventually got my own class teaching seasoned firefighters. I was eager, gung-ho and ready to go! The very first end of the class review stated "has no business teaching." That is what can happen! It was devastating for me, because I cared; I put all of my effort into what I was doing. Several years later, I may still not be any good but I've been given the chance to teach multiple times at the largest fire service conference in the country (Fire Department Instructors Conference) and even given the chance to work in the private sector with groups like Rockwell Automation (as a speaker – the irony, right?). Just last week I left a college level lecture and afterwards was offered a teaching position on the spot. What I learned from the first review was to study even the ugliest comment and if you can turn that individual to the positive, you have done something.

Giving Up is Not an Option

In Georgia there is a coveted, advanced firefighter program that requires a grueling acceptance test before you even begin the program. After nearly 30 years, there are just over 1000 graduates and has become a standard across the country for advanced firefighter training. The Georgia Smoke Divers (GSD) slogan is "Strong in Mind and Body." This program requires you to not only be physically fit but study adamantly various topics and to keep a sane mind while operating in less than ideal environments. After training for months, studying books every day and implementing a brutal physical fitness program – I failed the qualification test half way through. I was unable to complete a particular drill in the specified time limit. I had two options; forget it, because it had no effect on my current job, pay, promotions, or any other adverse effects to my current livelihood. But, I could not let it go - it affected my heart and my ability to drive forward. I took the hard road and learned from what I failed at and became stronger for it. On the second qualification test, nearly a year later I was accepted and completed the course on my first attempt; on the first attempt with the same teammate I started with. It was God's grace that allowed us to learn each other's strengths and weaknesses very quickly and receive the black t-shift and GSD #741.

Throughout life there are going to be failures and these were just a few that stand out in my mind. Don't ever give up, dream big, and drive forward. I heard a sermon recently that said God blesses the prepared mind. No one prays to not be broke into, but leaves their door unlocked. Prepare for what you are attempting to accomplish and finish the drill!

Key Points:

- Face adversity head on.

- Use the situations as experiences.

- Listen first.

- Do not hit reply all.

- Have tough skin and do not let others make decisions for you.

- Failure is a learning tool. Learn to accept failure as a character builder and never give up.

Chapter 9

"Personal Mastery is the phrase we use for the discipline of personal growth and learning. People with high levels of personal mastery are continuously expanding their ability to create the results in life they truly seek."

Peter Senge

It's a New Generation

You're One of Them

Shortly after I arrived at my current department I was addressing a group from the production side of the industrial facility on the hazards of hydraulic oil and the cost we were incurring from basically a lack of attention to detail. I attempted to explain the issue, the why, and the benefits; and how we were wishing to recognize employees who assisted the facility. As I wrapped up I asked if there were any questions and could I count on them? One 25 year veteran looked up from the back and wanted to provide some disruption by saying "Why should we trust you, you are one of them?" You have very few options at this point and my choice was to simply say I can't help what happened before me but we can move forward if we work together. Six months later I was asked to accept leadership for this production department (completely outside of my comfort zone – remember accepting the tough assignments) in addition to my previous duties. This very same veteran I later promoted to a formal leadership role within the department. The transformation could have went either way. It is all based in the principles of handling adversity and developing employees. I could have replied back because I said so or expressed that his comment didn't matter, however, neither of these responses would have built the relationship.

This is a good point to review generational differences. As a Barn Boss you must understand the station dynamics of the behaviors within your team. If you study and understand these differences you will be able to provide solutions and guide your team through training, adversity, and everyday operations. I commonly discuss the turning point in our society where we have two extremes clashing, when they shouldn't be, and most of us are stuck in the middle. There is the experience, tried and true veterans who learned the "why" from years of trial and error; then, there is the new science and technology rich generation coming up with a different perspective of the "why." We will not be as successful as we could be if the generational differences are not put aside. It will take both perspectives for us to reach the optimal capability. I need the veterans to teach me their "why" and provide me the historical perspectives and I need the new science "why" to help me put all of the pieces together.

A New Pair of Shoes

My father was a very old school individual who grew up working on the farm and dropping out of school to help take care of the family. He eventually completed his high school requirements and entered the Navy as a Boiler Technician on the USS LAW – Destroyer, where he spent most of his time. The Navy allowed him to travel the world and see places and things most of us will never see, however, he didn't grow up with much and appreciated the little things he had. This carried over into my childhood through many examples, however, one story I feel really tells the difference between the old and new generations. I was about 13 at the *time and it was the back to school shopping where you pick out your supplies and buy needed clothes, etc... It was our family tradition (or at least mine) to get a new pair of shoes for school. We did our shopping and I finally convinced my mother that I needed this one particular pair of Nike shoes. They were black with white lettering and said AIR in big letters on the side. They were even Hi-Tops, which provides additional ankle support or so I told my mom (she always wanted me to be safe). We made the purchase and within 20 minutes of being home my father looked at the receipt and sent my shoes back. The added ankle support agreement he didn't care much about, however the $100 price tag he did. The shoes represented materials and materials are not important. Although devastated at the time, my wife now tells me I'm the same way and materials mean nothing in a world full of materialistic people. This is a prime example of generational differences being exhibited through the environments we grew up in.*

Generation What?

Several years ago I was looking through a list of classes for a symposium coming up and there it was, "New Generation: Is it killing us?" I paused for a minute and asked myself, "Who is the New Generation and why are they killing firefighters?" Now, I have listened to Chief Billy Goldfeder and Chief Rick Lasky talk about veterans and company officers trying to relate with the rookies coming on board at the station and trying to get them to buy stock and take pride in their station. So, I came to the conclusion that it was it being suggested that my generation was killing firefighters. Through observations and comments made all around us, you commonly hear things such as, "Them kids these days..." Alan Brunacini even provided that his elders spoke the same words in 1958 to him as a rookie. He also provided that each generation seems to see the same history repeat itself. With a little research, I found that I am the New Generation (at the time), Generation X / Y – I'm in that hybrid stage.

Now, I believe that it's quite odd that a Generation can be killing firefighters. I did not attend the class and I'm not sure what it's about, but the title did its job and caught my attention. Some of you will believe whole heartily that "Them kids" are killing us, but let's look at a couple of things before we go too far on that. Looking at backgrounds can be revealing. I typed in Generations Y and X, just to see what it pulled up on the internet. I received a list of several Generations. There was the Lost, GI, Silent, Baby Boomers, X, MTV, Y, and newest edition Z Generation. Every one of the generations grew up in a different environment and atmosphere. Take the GI Generation, they had to fight for this country in WWII, and that is what they did. The Baby Boomers grew up with the 60's lifestyle, but somehow became more conservative later in life, go figure. Generation X dealt with the end of the Cold War and saw the fall of the Soviet Union. They were commonly associated with "dislike for authority and disrespect for their parents." Finally, Generation Y grew up with the World Trade Center, internet, video games and God being taken out of everything we do.

Each generation was brought into a unique environment, but there are individuals that succeed and fail from each. The ones that succeeded know what they had to endure to get here, knowing that there are a lot worse places to be and no one will take that away. I believe that it is a just a trend in the grand scheme of things. When the Baby Boomers were coming up, I'm pretty sure that their parents said "Heaven help us if they ever run this country!" My parents didn't have to worry about me running the country; they just wanted to get me out of high school. I can say that there are some lack luster personnel (commonly referred to by more descriptive terminology) that come into the Fire Service every day and a lot of them do not know how to work, the difference between pain and hurt, or how to push themselves. They have never had a job or had to support themselves, and they never had to eat Ramen Noodles for weeks at a time. Perfect example of what I commonly have seen with my generation, using a chain saw growing up was common place for me; most of the people coming into the service today barely know which end cuts. Or, the favorite newbie job of bathroom duty and they have to be shown what Windex is. I don't say that to be cruel or anything else, if they haven't been introduced to it, how can they be expected to know it. As I was saying earlier, I am a part of the Generation X/Y time period. So, how can I accurately assess my own Generation? I believe it has more to do with the environment you were brought up in than anything else.

Most of the lifelong task skills I developed were built out of necessity for maintaining our land, growing the garden, and putting food on the table. My brothers and I also learned how to problem solve early on. There would be a task that our dad would want to accomplish and he expected it to be complete when he came home. He did not always give the most concise and descriptive directions so we had to anticipate what he would do and our father never half-way completed a job. It was over kill or not at all – we once built a porch on the back of house simply because he wanted to lower the

> *"I did not always appreciate these teachings, as it was many years later when I found the value in these accomplishments."*

AC bill. So, we built a 14' x 70' covered porch with hurricane straps, 4" x 6" roof timbers, and 6" x 6" post placed on 8" footers – 24" deep. When the apocalypse comes, I'll be on the porch. This was one of many large scale tasks as a child that we accomplished as a family, there's still the two car garage, the apartment, the front porch, chicken coops, and sheds that were built with child labor – his child's labor and our payment was dinner. I did not always appreciate these teachings, as it was many years later when I found the value in these accomplishments. Hara Estroff Marano, A Nation of Wimps, describes experience development as this: A child's opportunity to learn problem solving and experience opportunities for themselves requires them to use their own inner resources, test their own limits, and develop confidence in themselves. If they don't, they become fragile and shatter easily – they become teacup kids. And, teacup kids become teacup adults.

In a 2008 study by the University of Pennsylvania with West Point students at the US Military Academy it was determined that "Grit" was a better indicator of military academy success than any other variable by itself. This included SAT scores, high school rank, athletic achievements/experience, and faculty appraisal scores. It is believed that "Grit" is closely tied to passion and commitment for the long haul. These individuals are not put down by short term struggles and they can endure most setbacks. There is also the mix of emotions, passion, and optimism for completion which intertwine to develop what is described as "Grit."

It may be inferred and correctly so, I was raised in the middle of nowhere, and life was simple. My typical days growing up consisted of cutting grass from the time I weighed enough to hold the springs down (some will understand without further explanation), chopping wood, and mixing "mud" for a Brick Mason at the age 14 for $5 an hour. Not because I was pushed to but because it meant independence, it was something bigger than what I was. The real motive was if I was paying for the truck, insurance, gas, etc… How could my parents take it away? It was a growing opportunity for me to learn many different experiences, take a pick – financial, punctuality, work ethic, team work, etc…. Looking back it wasn't much money but it was enough for me! That was what I was brought up in, my older brothers worked the same way, and my parents expected all of us to carry our name proudly, sure we all made our mistakes but we learned from them. Whatever you do, do 110%, even scrubbing the toilet. Think about it this way, if your crew can't trust you to simply clean the bathroom, how can they trust you on the fire ground.

What do Helicopters, Hothouses and Snowplows have in Common?

There are several terms thrown around today including helicopter parents, the hothouse, and snowplow parents. The helicopter parents hover around everything their children do and makes a lot noise – such as the parent who visited the fire academy because they didn't like how the push-ups were being completed. The hothouse parent's bottle up their children's ability to explore and learn the world, they typically fail to develop communication skills with those outside of their inner circle. Finally, the snowplow parents try to plow down everything for their prince or princess, such as showing up to the job interview in an attempt to assist answering the questions for them.

While everyone wants their children to succeed we all have to face the real world. We all have to be prepared to fight for what we have earned. It is beyond the scope of this text to dive into the societal issues, but I would encourage leaders to diversify. Study the differences (not just your opinion) between societies as a whole including the different generations.

Case in point: typically I arrived at the station 45 – 60 minutes before shift change mainly to get my stuff in order and to get mentally ready for the day. As well, if the crew was up all night they would appreciate someone taking the late call for them – if you have a habit of clocking in one minute before, change your ways now. By arriving early, you build a comradery with the other shifts and can really stifle any shift wars from occurring. You also learn from what occurred the day before and receive valuable pass-on information. I digress, back to the main point, I typically arrived early and every morning I would see these marker ticks on the whiteboard. Sometimes it even made it into the roman numerals dictations. For the first little while, I didn't think much of it and passed it off as members paying for chow, etc… Until one morning, members of both shifts were gathered in the day room and one of the rookies made a comment starting with the infamous "My daddy" and then you would see one of the veterans slick as night place another tick on the whiteboard. It all clicked at this moment as his father was a well-respected officer in our department. As this unfolded a couple of thoughts came to mind – 1) Did he never realize the ticks on the board shift after shift? Maybe his situational awareness was flawed. 2) He obviously was not aware of how he was being perceived or the words that were coming out of his mouth. 3) It is fine to be proud of

your family, but be careful to not ride on their coat tails, pave your
own path.

Connecting the Generations

One thing that can be accomplished is finding a way to
connect, from the veterans to the rookies. We have to close that gap.
Rookies need to be in everyone's back pocket, absorbing as much
knowledge as they can handle. The veterans need to remember that
the performance of your crew is based on your leadership, so share
your knowledge. The biggest aspect that I remember in my first
years was Company Officers taking an interest in my career and
what I wanted to do with it. I was pushed to be great at what I did,
sub-par wasn't an option and it was known. With that I made my
mistakes, but you learn from them and you move on, you Grow Up!
Not everyone is going to have the luxury of having a great Company
Officer, some are just there to collect a paycheck. That is when you
have got to learn to step up and step out on your own. For people
entering the Service, keep in mind that people may tell you getting
an education is worthless; if you do extra work, you're just brown
nosing, etc… But, believe me it's worth sticking to your guns
because it will make a difference in the end. Ultimately, if one thing
that you passed on saved a heart ache then it's all worth it and that's
the responsibility of all generations.

Generational Differences in the Fire House

January 2016, Fire Rescue Magazine published my article "Bridging the Gap," this article outlined the differences of the generations in the Fire House. It also dove tailed into understanding the context of each generation and how to bring all generations together. This is a constant topic brought up, whether it is in my training officer or officer development workshops. So, if you think this is just a daunting task for you specifically, it is not. There are a

"There are a tremendous amount of connections, context, background, and environments which affect how every group dynamic works together."

tremendous amount of connections, context, background, and environments which affect how every group dynamic works together. The bad news is that there is not a one size application or formula to fit all situations. As a leader, there are several items which you need to be able to pick up on, decipher what it means, and learn the characteristics of your people.

There are many assumptions made concerning why it is difficult to mesh generations with most being subjective and judgmental. For example, "kids just don't know how to work these days" or "Captain is just old and crusty stuck back 100 years." These are all perceptions, however, there is some truth to what is spoken – we, as officers/leaders, should understand the context of the situation describing the different generations. We (humans) typically criticize what we do not know or understand. Understanding this context allows us to have appreciation for the various generations and capitalize on the strengths of each. On the Fire Engineering Website "Training Officer's Toolbox: Influence" lesson, it depicts in a very few words how officers are leaders and need to understand the influence they place on their crews by taking advantage of each members strengths and developing their weaknesses.

Looking at the matrix below you are able to quickly identify a few key trends, however, I'll be the first to warn you – do not stereotype. If you learn the characteristics of your crew there is no need to stereotype. However, what we will discuss below is a blended approach to incorporate all generations based on general assumptions of where each group's strength is typically represented. The generations used in this matrix include Traditionalist, Baby Boomers, Generation X and Generation Y (Traditionalist may be referred to as Veterans in some text and for the purpose of this chapter Generation Z is included in Gen Y).

Culture, experience, background, environment, and education are just a few of the different types of factors which can affect personality traits of any generation. The key factor for any leader is to use a multi-pronged approach when working with crew so that there is a cognitive, psycho-motor and affective domain involvement. This ensures that knowledge is delivered (cognitive); there was a hands-on portion (psycho-motor) and the "why" was discussed to connect with the audience (affective). In the Training Officer's Desk Reference, David Wall discusses the learning styles associated with various generations including the Gen Y, Gen X, Baby Boomer and Traditionalist. Each of these provide several challenges when you consider their individual learning styles, blending these learning styles and retaining the attention span of each in the same setting.

Generational Matrix

The Generational Matrix on the following pages discusses how to combine these learning styles and generations based on my research and experiences as a professional trainer in the public and private sector. It also discusses assumptions with each generation, which should be considered for all generations as there are no "exacts" in generational research. In a presentation type of situation the leader should learn to read the audience and understand these general assumptions.

Note: All of these are generalities and there are no exacts to generations. Point of Reference to consider - Vets and Baby Boomers mostly grew up with tools in hand performing manual labor; Gen X and Gen Y mostly grew up with data and IT in hand performing brain exercises. (The Pendulum has swung to the exact opposite, however, it does not mean that neither can adapt).

General Assumptions (Gen X and Y): Technology driver; must keep engaged; they use science and data to understand the "Why"

General Assumptions (Veterans and Traditionalist): Tons of experience and knowledge; understand historical perspectives; Provide the "Why" based on Trial and Error; Just Do It!

Generational Matrix			
	Gen Y	Gen X	Baby Boomer	Veteran/ Traditionalist
Gen Y	Team Teach; Create Video; Tell the Why; CBT w/ HOT follow-up; Allow to pick any topic; Must keep engaged	Team Teach; Create Video; HOT; Demonstration; Both Tech Savvy	Gen Y provides lesson; Baby Boomer Facilitates and adds key notes; HOT; Gen Y uses technology to emphasize	Gen Y provides lesson; Vet facilitates and adds key notes; Vet takes lead on advance/technical materials; HOT
Gen X	Team Teach; Create Video; HOT; Demonstration; Both Tech Savvy	Team Teach; Allow SME to Lead; Demonstration; HOT; Tech Savvy	Baby Boomer provides historical background; Gen X provide technology; Great Knowledge for Demonstration	Vet provides historical background; key insights; Gen X provides the why and technology
Baby Boomer	Gen Y provides lesson; Baby Boomer Facilitates and adds key notes; HOT; Gen Y uses technology to emphasize	Baby Boomer provides historical background; Gen X provide technology; Great Knowledge for Demonstration	Discussion; HOT; Semi-Circle with equipment; Flip Charts and Whiteboard; Teach anything w/ experience	Discussion; use expertise of Vets; Lots of knowledge and experience; Use Flip Chart and whiteboard; Teach anything w/ experience
Veteran / Traditionalist	Gen Y provides lesson; Vet facilitates and adds key notes; Vet takes lead on advance/technical materials; HOT	Vet provides historical background; key insights; Gen X provides the why and technology	Discussion; use expertise of Vets; Lots of knowledge and experience; Use Flip Chart and whiteboard; Teach anything w/ experience	Discussion; use expertise of Vets; Lots of knowledge and experience; Use Flip Chart and whiteboard; Teach anything w/ experience

Melissa Dittmann describes these generational challenges in a team-building scenario which could very well represent your firehouse or fire academy. Melissa accurately describes what each generation thinks of the other. These generational differences are obstacles which we have to overcome when combining generations.

"Boomers may believe gen Xers are too impatient and willing to throw out the tried-and-true strategies, while gen Xers may view boomers as always trying to say the right thing to the right person and being inflexible to change. Traditionalists may view baby boomers as self-absorbed and prone to sharing too much information, and baby boomers may view traditionalists as dictatorial and rigid. And, gen Xers may consider millennials too spoiled and self-absorbed, while millennials may view gen Xers as too cynical and negative."

The following information was derived from the American Psychological Association as generalities when considering the various generations. As you think through the time periods try to consider what culture and backgrounds they encountered growing up as this explains a good portion of how and why they think the way they do (ex. WWII, Cuban Missile Crisis, Desert Storm):

It is very common in today's society that you may receive a 18 – 28 year old recruit who grew up in a suburb or downtown where there is limited opportunities to use tools common to the fire service. For example, generally speaking there are very few trees to cut down where everything is paved. As well, there is no need for mechanical aptitude if there is nothing to work on (tractors, small engines, making your Go-Kart really fast, etc.). Simply due to the environment which an individual grows up in will greatly affect what they bring to the table in the beginning. However, there are other characteristics and traits which will assist these individuals succeeding in other areas. And, they may very well adapt to this new fire service environment with no issues at all. The point to the story is to not judge based on the generation but understand their experiences, background and cultures – it will give you a different perspective.

Traditionalist: (Before 1945) – These individuals can be described as hard working, family/community oriented, and their motivation was internal self-worth. Their love for their homeland was second to none and they understand what it means to be an American as they fought through WWII. These individuals were also very personable due to everything being handled with a handshake and a conversation (Grew up with tools in hand and during great depression).

Baby Boomers: (1946-1964) – These individuals are the reason for long hours and the "work until it is done" mentality. They were very similar to the traditionalist in the personable skills and later in life technology made a major impact (First colored TV marketed in 1950s and the Cuban Missile Crisis occurred in 1962). Most Baby Boomers grew up learning from their parents who taught them work ethic and hard work pays off.

Generation X: (1965-1980) – "I" prefer competency based versus time based – if I can complete the task to perfection in two hours do I still need to sit through all 8-hours. "I" also like time off and money is not as important as living. Technology really became a major factor during this time generation (MTV, internet, email, and video); however, they did see international conflict during Desert Storm. They challenge status quo – not to be disrespectful but to understand why.

Generation Y: (1979-2006) – Generation Y likes to be different, as individuality is important to them. They tend to look at "today's" pay-off and work as a means to live. Children under the age of five are learning to turn on and play games on their PCs. This generation can create PowerPoint presentations and develop IMovie Videos with narration embedded into the PowerPoint with multimedia simulations. They also question the "why" as fire science has made many strides and our school systems are teaching numerous theories in many classes. Check out the ridiculousness of common core math.....

Putting it All Together

A few years ago, as a 25-year-old training officer, I overheard a conversation from my officers concerning the implementation of an incident safety officer course. As a Gen X/Yer (solid foundation with technology and challenge the status quo for the "why" mentality), I took the initiative to study the materials and develop the course for our command level officers (including completing the NFA ISO and FDSOA ISO certification). However, I knew that I would need help and that I did not have the experience to teach the tactical perspective of the ISO position. In response to this, I solicited the knowledge of well-respected 20+ year Captain Wayne Mooney (now Deputy Chief) and he delivered the tactical considerations. Chief Mooney (Baby Boomer Mentality – hard work, steadfast, and experienced) appreciated the initiative and work ethic associated with me driving this program. This team attack approach from opposite generations worked well as we gained a lot of respect for each other as well as learned from each other. The key for us was to be open-minded and forget the "it's always been done this way" or the "it's my way or no way."

"It's always been done this way"

In-Service Training

The above example is just one way of describing how two different generations can work together. The key is understanding the strengths and weaknesses of each individual applying what it is that they bring to the table. In my officer development course I provide a training scenario at the fire station with multiple generations involved and have them develop a plan for incorporating all of the individuals. Attempt this at your station:

You have decided to provide a fire behavior class to an in-service crew consisting of the following (below) – be prepared to discuss your thought process for incorporating those below (the expectation is that they are all actively involved):

6 month Probie

10 year Engineer

15 year Lt.

22 year Capt.

35 year Batt. Chief

Suggestion

There is no right or wrong answer per say, however, I offer the following suggestion. The beauty of this flow is that everyone is actively learning prior to being provided the actual lesson. As well, if you read between the lines, there is a mentorship being developed without any formal mentoring program (how it is supposed to happen). Each generation is able to capitalize on what they do best – which creates fulfillment and a sense of accomplishment. Due to all of the frontend work, once the class is delivered the discussions should go beyond the basics and provide realistic decision-making applications.

6 month Probie: Develops the actual PowerPoint/lesson plan after researching the topic using any means they see fit (let them explore). They could also create a video for the lesson using one of the many free video software's such as IMovie or Windows Movie Maker. The probie should also be prepared to speak through the PowerPoint and review with the 22-year captain or 35-year battalion chief for the experience perspective.

10 year Engineer: This individual should review the lesson plan and develop a hands-on activity that works to emphasize the points stressed in the probie's presentation. Prior to the class, review with the probie what activity is being planned so they understand how to speak to the lesson/activity. This individual is also very tech savvy so they could assist with the research or video development.

15 year Lieutenant: The role of the 15-year Lieutenant is to work with the 10-year engineer to ensure that the appropriate resources are available for the activity. They should offer suggestions as well as provide any experience that may lend to assisting in understanding the topic.

22 year Captain / 35 year Battalion Chief: These roles know the "why" due to their experience and knowledge surrounding the topic. They should play active roles in offering subtle suggestions for adding practicality and realism to the lesson and the hands-on activity. These individuals should allow the others involved to take the lead however provide "words of wisdom" to fill in gaps or where opportunities present themselves to expand on the topic.

Remember, your team is only as strong as the weakest link and no one deserves to be left behind. The challenge for those reading this book is to ensure everyone is involved and regardless of the generation or background of an individual, everyone can create value. True leaders understand how to challenge, yet mentor, each generation in order to develop them and capitalize on the strengths of each team member. Generational differences are a great thing and provide us with numerous opportunities to help us all grow.

Key Points:

- Learn the strengths and weaknesses of those around you.
- Leverage the strengths and develop the weaknesses as a team.

- Use the generational matrix to assist blending different generations.
- Attempt to understand the different perspectives which developed the various generations. This will provide insight into how they think, react, and what motivates them.
- Do not fall into the "it's always been done this way trap."

Chapter 10

"The challenge of leadership is to be strong, but not rude; be kind, but not weak; be bold, but not bully; be thoughtful, but not lazy; be humble, but not timid; be proud, but not arrogant; have humor, but without folly."

Jim Rohn

Article Series - Leadership From the Little Guy:

What it takes to be the Informal Leader!

Have you ever considered what it takes to be a leader in your department? How much of an influence or change agent can an individual be without the use of trumpets or 30 years of seniority? Have you ever considered what it takes to make a change in the fire service? The fact of the matter is that anyone can provide the push for changes to take place in our service. The key is to understand and practice certain characteristics that will exemplify who you are and show what you stand for.

In this section we will discuss many different topics; however, the majority of our discussion will revolve around a four step process that I have found beneficial to my development in the service. Although I may mention some theory, I do not claim to be a leadership theorist, the basis of what I will discuss is how I accomplished different task in my career. Maybe this could be called the School of Hard Knocks Leadership, it was a learning process, but a process that none-the-less has proven well.

Before we dive off into the four step process though, I want you to think about leaders in general. What makes you think of them as leaders? What traits bring about your respect for them? A small sample of some of the traits that people commonly tie to leaders include: Knowledge, Understanding, Competence, Decisiveness,

Trustworthiness, Sympathy, and Tactfulness to name just a few. There are many more but these seem to be common in most circles. As Former City of Atlanta Fire Chief Kelvin Cochran states, "There is no cookie cutter style of leadership, each individual has to develop their own authentic leadership to be successful."

As we realized, the items that we discussed in the last paragraph provided no direct linkage to any rank or seniority. Then, "in theory," it could hold true that a younger, maybe moderately experienced firefighter could have the capacity to lead a group of individuals to great things if this individual possessed these certain traits. Now, with this in mind, how do we develop these particular traits? Some of these are learned over time such as life experience and/or experience on the job, as one grows one learns. Some of these experiences are even forced on us. Early on for me I had to make a decision whether to hang out with friends or go to work when I was in high school due to my father becoming disabled. I did not necessarily appreciate having to do this at the time but the work ethic developed has proven to be a great asset in this profession.

Job experience can come from simply asking for the busy station assignments. These types of assignments will allow you to build confidence in your decisions through repetition. Foremost, as you develop your skill level and make improvements, you will gain respect for your actions. After spending 2.5 years as a training officer for GCFES, one of my deciding factors in leaving the fire academy was to obtain more field experience. Within the first few months of being assigned to one of our busiest stations I saw more "awkward" calls then I had seen in quite some time. The other added benefit to this was that I was riding as the officer on calls such as a Haz Mat Suicide, Industrial Accident, the infamous Man on Fire, and multiple homicides. All of these were certainly challenges, but they are the calls that will aid in developing anyone's problem-solving and decision making skills.

I do find it necessary to share a quote that I have come to admire. The quote comes from the Father of the Fire Service, Benjamin Franklin. He stated that "Experience keeps a dear school, but fools will learn in no other." Francis Brannigan added to this statement by saying, "In the Fire Service the price of experience is blood and grief." As an individual grows, we cannot rely solely on experience. We have to expand our education and knowledge beyond just what we can see and do it before the call comes in. It may be the training or education that prepares us to handle one of these awkward calls, and may just prevent an injury or death.

So far, everything that we have talked about concerns methods for learning the traits and characteristics that are needed to become effective leaders. One of the other primary aspects of this includes the use of mentoring and specifically looking at the "Two Perspective Approach to Mentoring." The two perspectives come from the Mentee and the Mentors point of view. As the mentee, we all need to be looking for the individuals that can provide us with knowledge and advice on different situations. As the Mentor, we all need to be willing to provide this knowledge and advice in order to grow the organization and the individual skills of the mentee. During a presentation by FDNY Retired Deputy Chief John Norman, he described the importance of leaving behind a legacy in your organization and further explains how mentoring helps accomplish this. The ability to embrace multiple mentorships with proven leaders (formal or informal) will allow an individual to grow in multiple directions and manifest their ability to develop different perspectives (or solutions) to particular situations (or problems).

Moving forward, after understanding what it takes to develop these traits and characteristics, it's time to mention the four step process. This process includes: Vision, Proactive, Action-Oriented, and Demonstrator of Beliefs.

Vision

No individual can move forward in any capacity in life without a vision. We can all live day to day but we will never accomplish anything without the ability to look beyond what is in front of us. The philosophy of Vietnam Veteran Lieutenant General Hal Moore, A.K.A. Mel Gibson in "We Were Soldiers," was to always ask himself what more could he be doing. Once he realized what he should be doing, he continued to look farther and farther down the road. He always felt there was more that he could or should be doing. Don't stop with the present, always look to the future.

Proactive

Being proactive is directly related to your vision. If you are able to visualize, then you have the ability to be proactive, whether you choose to use it or not. You have the ability to do before told or before an event occurs. With all of the situations and circumstances facing the fire service such as line-of-duty-deaths and on-the-job injuries there are plenty of things that we need to be proactive with. Waiting until something tragic happens is not the time to decide to do something.

Action-Oriented

Action-Oriented simply means leading by example. Be the individual that people look up to, talk less and mean more. Another way of putting it is to let your actions speak for who you are. Along with this you must challenge yourself beyond the minimum acceptable standard. It's not "good enough" to be just the minimum. I cannot recall who said it but the quote states "It's great that you passed the promotional test with a 93, but I want to know what 7 percent of your job you don't know." This exemplifies what being Action-Oriented is, going above and beyond.

Demonstrator of Beliefs

Being a Demonstrator of Beliefs goes hand in hand with being Action-Oriented. However, going above and beyond does not mean that you believe in what you are doing. This means to not only do and say but to truly understand why we do and say. No matter what you try to do or accomplish, show that your heart is in everything that you do. Even people that may normally be against a certain initiative, if they know that it's coming from what's inside you they will be much more receptive to listening to you.

Vision: Visualizing Your Future Fire Service

In the first section we focused the majority of our discussion on the characteristics and traits of effective leaders. As we moved through the article, I described a four step process that I found vital to my career and my development as an *"Preparing Today, In Order To Lead Tomorrow."* informal leader. The first step we will discuss is Vision: Visualizing Your Future Fire Service. As previously stated, no individual can move forward in any capacity of life without a vision. We can make it day to day but we will never accomplish our dreams or, more importantly, live to our full potential. It really just comes down to the theme that I used for my first leadership conference, *"Preparing Today, In Order To Lead Tomorrow."*

Webster's Dictionary defines vision as, "A thought, concept or object formed by the imagination; unusual discernment or foresight." All successful leaders have a vision for what we need but don't have and what we need to be doing that we are not. These leaders are not blinded by the forest when looking through to the trees. Classic examples include Martin Luther King Junior's vision - dream of peace and John F. Kennedy's putting a man on the moon. These individuals had a drive that pushed them to achieve goals for the greater good of mankind. What made them different than anyone of us? The answer is their vision.

The fire service has faced many obstacles, even in my short career. These obstacles can prove to be disheartening and crushing to people that have worked tirelessly for the betterment of our departments. However, these individuals do not go away, they do not quit, and they do not give up. It is their vision for a greater good, a better fire service, and the development of a philosophy that will send everyone home at the end of the day that drives them. From the time that I finished my first basic firefighter course I was never satisfied with the status quo. I was never satisfied with where I was as a firefighter. However, it was not that I was discontent with any organization or individually, it was my craving to know more and to be better than what I currently was. I have heard the comments such as "You'll burnout" or "You'll get tired someday," but I'm pleased to say that this desire still remains. As well, each accomplishment drives the next goal.

One of the first visions that I had was the creation of the Gwinnett County Leadership and Safety Conference. It started out after a meeting with the area training officers concerning training that needed to be created for our departments. The concept for the conference is very simple, if I could bring in one speaker to train a few of us, why not bring in numerous speakers to train a whole lot of us. In addition, if I could get some assistance to pay for it then we could train even more firefighters. It all started with looking at FDNY Battalion Chief John Salka to conduct a Rapid Intervention class, this was a heavy topic at the time. After adding a couple of sponsors, Retired FDNY Deputy Chief John Norman, Fire Chief Rick Lasky and a few others, our first conference was born with 250 firefighters attending. No one in the Atlanta area had done such a thing, at least not in my time, of this magnitude. In essence, there was no template or tremendous assistance as far as advice to guide this project. Everything, good and bad, came from the vision that was trapped inside my head.

I think that this is what Vietnam Veteran Lieutenant General Hal Moore was talking about during the 2007 American Veterans Center Conference. His philosophy of always asking himself what more could he be doing and once he realized this, what else could he be doing. This is the positive effect of having a vision. This was probably a large contributing factor to him surviving the war.

One of the benefits of having a vision is the resultant plan that formulates from the development of your vision. Having the ability to organize, prioritize, and manage your workload comes from the creation of steps that lead to your end goal. In order for us to reach this particular goal, there are always steps that must be taken first. This is best described by saying that as we accomplish the little task, the big picture becomes much clearer and the image is greatly enhanced. In essence, as Mark A. Hinz states it, "A vision makes a possibility, a reality."

When talking about an individual's vision, specifically career enhancement and professional development, the establishment of goals is vital to success. Establishing goals, or benchmarks as we call them in the fire service, will identify several items. The first item needing to be identified is knowing where you want to be in 25 or 30 years. Making this decision now does not mean that it cannot be changed mid-way through; however, it will create options for you when that time comes. The second item is the creation of a time line or a prioritization chart. Start at the 30 year mark and begin listing items that will help you accomplish your end goal. It is generally best to use a year to year format for the short term and then start a 5 year interval plan for the long term. Having this time line will keep you from freelancing and help you focus on particular items that are vital at each specific point in your career. The third item is to simply start with the first item on your list, as you accomplish them cross them off and continuously update your prioritization chart. If you are unsure of what it may take to reach your goal, look at individuals from around the country. I started and still do read the Bios of authors in all the books and articles that I read for credibility of the text but also to understand what put them in the place that they are.

One of my personal goals was to successfully complete the Georgia Smoke Diver Program. This is an intense 6 day course full of non-stop safety and survival, and advanced search techniques. I did not know what the outcome would be when I started training several months out but I knew that I wanted to be on the other end when I completed this journey. My vision of being successful each time I suited up to train and during each drill, kept me focused on what I had to accomplish each specific moment. There were definitely struggles along the way, but it was this focus on the little steps that led to me completing that sixth day of training on a positive note. The GSD Creed is worth stating, it exemplifies what it takes to carry out a vision, and it is worth reciting when you feel like giving up, quitting, or feel that an obstacle is to tough.

"If I persist, if I continue to try, if I continue to charge forward, I will succeed. I will not hear those who weep and complain, for their disease is contagious. The prizes of life are at the end of each journey, not near the beginnings, and it is not given to me to know how many steps are necessary in order to reach my goal. I will never consider defeat, and I will remove from my vocabulary such words as quit, cannot, unable, impossible, failure, and retreat, for these are the words of fools and cowards. When my thoughts beckon my tired body homeward, I will resist the temptation to depart. I will try again. I will make one more attempt to close with victory, and if that fails, I will make another. When others cease their struggle, then mine will begin, and my harvest will be full."

One of the items that I have come to realize with having a vision is that there is a domino effect. Each time I move forward with completing one of my goals, it opens up unexpected doors. In return, these unexpected doors opened other doors that I never thought about. As this happened, it caused me to modify my goals, all the while allowing me to move closer and closer to my long term goal.

The intent is that as you read through this article, you will examine your future. Where do you want to be in 5, 10 and 20 years? What will it take for you to accomplish this? What steps do you need to take now that will dictate where you are in 20 years? The individuals with this type of vision and the ones that carry out their plans are the individuals that create legacies in the fire service. Their work will live on well past the departure from their department, and will be referenced for years to come.

Exemplify the Meaning of Being Proactive

Now, we will talk about simply being proactive or exemplifying what it means to be proactive. In Steven Coveys, 7 Habits of Highly Effective People, Habit number 1 is to be Proactive. He states that we should take responsibility for ourselves and not to allow the people or environments around us to decide or influence the behavior which we portray. Our behavior is the one thing that we can control without any outside influences. Proactive individuals tend to navigate their behaviors towards items that they can change and don't dwell on the items they can't.

Throughout the fire service we can see trends occurring in every department. Many of us know and can see these items, such as the cultural mentalities and skill levels amongst department members, which need to be addressed. However, we commonly do not act upon these items until a tragic event, an injury or a death occurs. At this point we start to look for ways to amend or adopt a new blanket policy for everything from this point forward or commonly known as the Knee-Jerk Reaction. In essence, we get trapped in a repetitive reactive state. We tend to travel in circles trying to solve these issues.

This concept was illustrated through a conversation held several years ago. It was stated that if we could just slow down the pace of our department for even a short amount of time, we would be able to catch up and put all of the right procedures in place and ensure that everyone is on the same playing field. However, only the opposite has occurred to this point, we have increased our speed to the tune of about 200 additional firefighters and 7 or 8 additional stations. With the exponential growth that has been experienced it has become even more essential that we, as individuals and departments, become proactive.

So, how do we become proactive? Most firefighters are gung-ho about coming to work and take care of the stations and apparatus to a precision level unknown in most occupations. However, sometimes what gets us bogged down is time management and not knowing where to get the resources needed to be proactive. When this happens we tend to procrastinate or totally suspend all operations. One of the best ways to counter act this situation is to build a vast network of resources by attending conferences, stepping outside of your bay walls, and simply looking to see what others are doing.

One of the things that I learned during my time as a training officer with Gwinnett County was that I would never survive the fire academy if I waited until I was told to do something. I would like to think and I believe that my officers would agree that I made my living while at the fire academy on producing work in a very timely manner if not already having it when the topic was mentioned. While being the youngest member of the fire academy staff at the time, being proactive allowed me to be involved and considered the subject matter expert as Chief Wayne Mooney justified it, on several topics for my department.

The greatest benefit on a personal level was that I was allowed to teach parts of the program as it became part of the Acting Battalion Chief Program. If you remember the domino effect that I mentioned in the last article, this was one of them times. After completing the ISO Program, I was asked to revise our building construction class and create a level two instructor program for our department. One simple item in the beginning created a lasting impact. Three years later, I'm teaching all of these programs plus several more that I developed and that was implemented in our department.

Now, this did much more under the surface of simply teaching programs in our department. There are certainly several people smarter than me and much more capable than me with doing all of this. However, what it did allow was for a level of trust to be developed and that my department knew that they could depend on me. Most of this came from learning to manage my time wisely and my willingness to work beyond my job description. Basically, there was a job that needed to be done and someone needed to do it.

The second item mentioned earlier was the knowing where to simply get the resources for quick reference. Once you find the resources, you are able to spend less time searching and more time developing, which in turn aids in time management. The result of one of my professional and personal goals, not only getting a degree but I am the first in my family to receive a degree, helped me create the list of references that established the resources page on www.FireServiceSLT.com. As I have completed my associate and bachelor degrees in fire science, I developed a list of resources that I found beneficial to my research and projects. While some of these resources are very technical based, there are many that are very tactical based as well. As I gathered more resources, my time management only improved which improved the level of how proactive I could be. In one sense you become the go-to-guy or gal. It is worth mentioning that as you become more proactive pay particular attention to the quality and not the quantity.

An additional item that we will talk about throughout this text is the use of risk. Sometimes being proactive requires us to take a leap of faith with some items. When I created the first Gwinnett County Leadership and Safety Conference, I put a lot of my own time and financial backing behind the conference. There was a tremendous risk involved in attempting this endeavor. However, as one individual stated; when you risk big, you win big. Now, do not take this the wrong way with attempting foolish and unnecessary risk. The statement of "we shall risk a lot within a structured and calculated plan," is a valuable concept to remember.

This risk was a direct result of my willingness to be proactive and it was a risk that I was willing to take simply because I thought it could make a difference. Every year within the structured plan mentioned, there are benchmarks and breaking points that have to be met for the program to continue. It is essential that as an individual reviews and analyzes the situations that they can make a difference with, and create a structured and calculated plan that fits the vision that you are executing against.

As you finish reading this text think about the internal behaviors that we discussed that effect you as an individual and as firefighter. What does it really mean to exemplify the meaning of being proactive? Having the ability to transform your vision into changing the situations that you have control over is the first aspect of being proactive. Directly related to this is our ability to manage time effectively. Once we learn to manage our time it becomes easier to prioritize items and increases our level of production while being proactive. In order to learn time management skills, learn to write things down and place them in order of importance. And lastly, broaden your horizons and explore different avenues for collecting information. Know where to go to get valid information. An individual that can put all of these items together and manage them in an effective manner will become a proactive individual. Be careful to not underestimate the importance of all the essential items.

And, above all, be motivated because this is the greatest job in the world!

Action Oriented: Let Your Actions Speak

Up to this point we have talked about the thought processes of moving your behaviors into active motion. In this section we will simply look at being action oriented and what does that really mean. A quote that I like to use when talking about the importance of learning new things and training, "Learning is an active process, you don't just get it scratching your rear-end on the lounge chair." However, it's obviously the doing part behind everything that we have talked about.

Action-Oriented can stand for a lot of items from simply leading by example to being the individual that people look up too. Another way of putting it is to let your actions speak and define who you are. Along with this you must challenge yourself to go beyond the minimum acceptable standard. It's not "good enough" to be just the minimum. This exemplifies what being Action-Oriented is, going above and beyond.

Why do we do it?

As well, there are a lot of doers out there. Some do it because they have to, some because they were told to and some because they have the passion and desire to do so. Doing it for the right reasons means a lot in our business and ultimately the individuals that do it for the right reasons will have dividends paid to them when they least expect it. They will ultimately be better at their jobs for this very same reason, because there is that sense of caring and compassion for what we face. The individual that just goes through the motions will never have that sense of true pride for the job.

Who are the doers?

These different types of firefighters that I am talking about have already been described by a couple of chiefs. You can listen to Retired Lewisville, Texas Fire Chief Rick Lasky and Hanover County Division Chief Eddie Buchanan talk all day about the 5 percenters in the fire service. About half of these are on the fence and just need some motivation to get involved, the other half are virtually dead other than having a pulse. But, it's that 95 percent of firefighters that get the work done, that actually do the job (I actually refer to this concept as the 80/10/10 rule earlier in the book based on the Pareto Rule). Within this, just as there are the negative 5 percenters, I would argue to say that there are 5 percent that become the leaders and motivators for accomplishing these task. These are the "Movers and Shakers" that you hear about. These are the individuals that are making a difference in their departments and the fire service as a whole. Bob Colameto, one individual that I have come to admire as a colleague and friend, exemplifies the meaning of this. I sat with Bob Colameta during the Congressional Fire Service Institute Dinner after he received the ISFSI/FDIC Instructor of the Year, where we had a long conservation about the fire service, teaching and having a passion for doing what we do. The thing that impressed me the most and what I learned was that Bob took the Program Manager's position with Everyone Goes Home; where he could affect a nation of firefighters over a (higher paying) chiefs position where he could only affect about 80 firefighters. I can only imagine how many firefighters that he has saved from injuries and fatalities, which neither he nor we will ever know about. This level of passion is truly remarkably. Bobby Halton provides the commentary, "As in most unpopular situations, lots of folks complain, but every now and then great men and women among us do more than that: They take action; they make a difference; and making a difference involves taking a risk, having a commitment to your virtues and principles and living up to that commitment."

The Impact!

There is another aspect to being action oriented, mainly the impact associated with execution of task(s). Talking less, means more. Look around the station at who is constantly talking and listen to what they are really saying. Do the words really make sense? Is there any validity behind what they are saying? Will they be listened to when it's crunch time?

One of the items that I didn't really have to strive for, it was kind of by default, but worked well for me was simply listening when people talked. Early on I quickly learned by watching others behaviors and you will start to identify the individuals that know what they are talking about. The individual that either complains or just rambles all day, what credit they may have is checked at the fire station door. It follows the same lines as the childhood story about the kid that always cried wolf when there wasn't one, and they discredited everything that the child said. When the town really needed to listen they didn't. The same rules apply in the fire station. However, the individual's that speak seldom and choose their words and battles wisely are quite often the ones listened to by the people that matter. They become the go-to-guy or gal because the officers know that they will shoot straight with them and simply not blow smoke. Furthermore, there is substance behind their words and their concepts.

Then again, sometimes it's just the simple actions that add respect to what you do. What happens to an individual when they are given a sense of entitlement or allowed to lead? I've always wondered how the hot air balloon fits on some people's shoulders. What I am trying to get across is the fact that just because you have some power doesn't mean that you always have to use it. Now, there are definitely times as a leader when it is imperative for the safety of your crew that you are decisive and forthcoming. However, these are only small percentages of the time. Think about the training officer that is teaching recruits how to test hose. I was involved with testing a large percentage of hose that belonged to the fire academy with the use of one of our recruit classes. After testing for 8 hours, they generally have the process down pretty good and it does become a tedious job. What is so wrong with helping the recruits roll and unroll the hose when you are talking about a job of this magnitude? However, I know instructors that wouldn't touch it. Due to this simple action who do you think the recruits are going to respect more? In essence, by participating what are your actions saying about you? On another note it's important to remember that the tail you kick today may be attached to the one you kiss tomorrow.

I also want to take a second and talk about doing what you say, which will lead into our next phrase, standing up for what you believe in. There are numerous people that you could talk about, who exemplify this: Goldfeder, Halton, and the list goes on. No matter who you are, your word is only as good as the action behind it. Talking about being safe and actually doing it are totally different. Simply writing this very statement can be tough. When Chief Wayne Mooney and I taught our ISO class, it is commonly discussed empowering firefighters to make a stand for safety. Simply allowing a two or three year firefighter to say "Hey, I'll back you up" or "Lt., Do you mind putting on your seatbelt?" These types of items can be extremely difficult to follow through on when you're talking to someone 20 years your senior, but do we need to do it? The answer is yes. If you are going to be given a platform to sell it, you better be willing buy it as well.

Appendix 1

This is the article that started it all when it was published on FireEngineering.com on Sept. 25, 2008. It was a great day in Tuscaloosa, Alabama at the Alabama Fire College, with no one to tell that the first article that I had ever submitted was just published – that's the way life goes sometimes.

Leadership From The Little Guy

What is leadership? Who shows leadership in your organization? By definition, a leader is someone who leads people toward a common goal. So, are you the Hitler or the Churchill of your organization? Both were effective leaders, but one of them was not leading for the right reasons.

But what made them leaders? If you asked 50 different people what leadership is, you would probably come up with 50 different answers, but all would probably agree on certain traits. Does anyone ever bring up rank or age as a leadership trait? Although these may be signs of someone that leads and has experience, they are not what make someone a leader.

A leader is decisive, strong, knowledgeable, cool, calm, and collected in times of disarray. We all want that strong command presence when we're working an incident. We want that understanding during troubled times. We want a leader that uses all of his traits, not his rank, to get respect.

With that said, a leader can easily be the little guy or gal with no rank. How many of us have seen someone that leads by example, steps out on the ledge to learn new material, does their job, goes to school, enhances his career beyond what is required, and expects nothing in return? Those are the marks of a leader. You must strive for more because no one will ever give you something for free.

There have been many newcomers in the U.S. fire service lately. A lot of these rookies are right out of high school; I've seen and heard of the many deficiencies in some of these personnel. Sometimes, it's basic things such as tying their shoes; sometimes it's more technical things, such as running a chain saw. But we have to find a way to bring them up. We have to empower our one-, two-, and three-year seasoned firefighters to become leaders in their own right. We must instill in them the traditions and the brotherhood of the fire service, as well as instruct them in the science of firefighting. We must teach them about building construction and structural collapse, and point out the Francis Brannigans, the Chief Vinnie Dunns, and others who have made contributed to fire science. They must learn about the origin of the Maltese Cross and the history behind the badge--it's not just a shiny piece of metal to wear.

Any member of the fire service can teach these lessons. You don't have to be a 20-year veteran to know the history behind the badge or why these subjects are important. You may be a two-year probie, but you can still have a powerful impact on the first day of a rookie. To all the inexperienced people, listen up, and to the already seasoned, lead by example. Don't be afraid to step out there, even if it is only in the station--a great starting point for developing leadership skills. General Robert E. Lee only promoted personnel that kept an orderly tent. Eventually, after you prove yourself, you have the opportunity to show what you can accomplish. Stick with it and show you can be responsible.

Appendix 2

"16 Life Safety Initiatives"

Saving Firefighter Lives One Initiative at a time….

A Gloves-Off Approach to Implementing the 16 Life Safety Initiatives!

What are you doing to make sure everyone is going home the same way they reported to work? Better yet… How about retiring with the same health they came on the job with? It's a tough assignment, but it's one that can be achieved with a little help. There are no more excuses. We're going to take a Gloves-Off, practical approach to implementing the 16 Firefighter Life Safety Initiatives, which doesn't require money, political bureaucratic BS that we have to be so delicate with or needing permission to be better at our job from anyone up the ladder. This is about the company officer and the firefighters taking care of each other and working together towards a common goal so we all go home in the morning. This is about a brotherhood taking care of each other.

As we go through these initiatives there are a couple of items that need to be made clear. There is no us and them, firefighters are just as responsible and capable as the company officers of being safety conscious and implementing these initiatives. If we can get buy-in from the higher ups on the ladder, the job just gets that much easier, but they are not necessary to implement. Don't look at all 16 and think they will appear tomorrow at your station. Pick the one or two that can create the biggest impact and focus on them. As you accomplish them move down to the next one with the biggest impact. God didn't create the Earth in a day; we're not going to save the world in a day either. Think about what an LODD would do to your department and your family.

Initiative #1: Define and advocate the need for a cultural change within the fire service relating to safety; incorporating leadership, management, supervision, accountability and personal responsibility.

A cultural change, it's easy to gripe about "them kids" or talk about them "smoke eaters" from the good ole days. But, what can we do to break the mold of these terms? Bridge the gap and start an informal mentoring program, nothing on paper or written down. If you're the firefighter find the individual that is always putting their hands on the tools even when it's not truck day. They will be the one that seems to always be in control and everyone looks to when times are tough. Get in their back pocket and suck up as much information as they will give you. Now, if you are the veteran or company officer find the new firefighter that is sitting around staring paint off the wall and make them put their hands on the tools with you. Talk to them about what is expected of them and how they can be a great asset and positively impact the organization. Another great example comes from Retired Chief Rick Lasky. He has an outstanding mentoring program where every person in his organization has three people they mentor, from firefighter to Chief.

Initiative #2: Enhance the personal and organizational accountability for health and safety throughout the fire service.

Simply give your firefighters an hour or two to work out and allow it between the 8 to 5 work schedules. This will accomplish a couple of items in the station. It will allow the individuals that want too but never have the time, to work out. It's contagious; once one starts others will start. If not, there's way to prod them into the gym or just get them to walk around the station for an hour. Then, if you're the company officer you need to lead by example and be out there at the same time, don't just sit behind the desk. This will do wonders for building your crews camaraderie. If you're the firefighter and none of the above works for your company officer, simply come into work early, get others to arrive a little early as well and you can still work out as a shift or wait until the evening and work out. The big point is to show you're committed to firefighters well-being and ask your company officer to join you, they just may. Lastly, don't just say the textbook answer of everyone's a safety officer. Give everyone in the station the tools to be a safety officer on-scene, teach them what to look for.

Initiative #3: Focus greater attention on the integration of risk management with incident management at all levels, including strategic, tactical, and planning responsibilities.

Poll your crew members and see how many understand or even know what Risk vs. Benefit is. Most will be surprised that a lot of people have either forgotten or were never taught the simple meaning of risk a lot to save a lot, risk a little to save a little and risk nothing to save what is already lost. There have been many modifications to this simple statement, most have added to it to make it more comprehensive. The easiest way to start learning is by sitting down at your shift meeting and review the IAFC "10 Rules of Engagement." Risk Management is something that we really do every day, we just never think about it. What we have to do is bring the components of RM to the front of our brains so we can make the most effective decisions on the incident. Review the components and learn how to use Risk Identification, Evaluation, Prioritization, Control Methods, and Monitoring.

Initiative #4: All firefighters must be empowered to stop unsafe practices.

We have reviewed some of this already with giving everyone the tools to be a safety officer on-scene. As a company officer it is important that you show your firefighters and explain to them that their opinion is valued. You may not always go with their decision but you should not criticize it either. Now if you're the firefighter don't wait until it's too late and something happens. Perfect example that happened to a colleague of mine involved him as a firefighter, his first fire, right out of recruit school. He remembered talking about fire behavior, backdrafts, and flashovers in recruit school but wasn't sure if he would recognize it or not if encountered. Short end of the story, he recognized the signs and then encountered a backdraft but choose not to say anything because he was the junior firefighter on-scene, as there were company and chief officers arriving on-scene. His thoughts were that he was inferior to everyone else on-scene. They were lucky; they finished evacuating just seconds before the backdraft occurred. Speak up and say something. A good program for helping implement this is Crew Resource Management which can be found on FireServiceSLT.com under the Training Page.

Initiative #5: Develop and implement national standards for training, qualifications, and certification (including regular recertification) that are equally applicable to all firefighters based on the duties they are expected to perform.

Although we are an advocate for what goes on at the national level we are going to focus on what goes on at the station level today. In 2009, I spent about $2,000 to attend a national conference and do you know what the big theme of the event was? "Back to the Basics." $2,000 to go back to the basics, it's sad but true. We are missing the boat in a lot of areas. A lot of firefighters don't understand how important training on our PPE, SCBA, Building Construction, and Fire Behavior are to us. Pull out the recruit manual and start reviewing all of these items. Make it fun but help everyone remember what to do in case of an emergency, how to operate the bypass, and what it feels like when the mask sucks to their face so they won't rip it off in a fire. This is just one item though and there are endless sources of information for everyone to use for training in different subjects. A good start would be to check out Fireengineering.com, let it be your daily newsfeed. Find something to train about every shift and in addition to that read something fire related every day for 15-20 minutes or find a fire service magazine, throw it on the kitchen table and dissect the incidents in it. Brian Kazmierzak, Director of Operations for Firefighter Close Calls, recently posted to his Twitter account him in a wet suit training, imagine the Chief of Training – doing training.

Initiative #6: Develop and implement national medical and physical fitness standards that are equally applicable to all firefighters, based on the duties they are expected to perform.

Until every fire department's administration understands how important it is to focus on our health we will have to do it on our own. First, check your insurance policy, most give you one free checkup a year. GO GET IT NOW. Recently, a brother of mine from up north went through several months of not feeling well and eventually came to the point where walking 100' in gear was wearing him out. He decided to get checked out and they found a 90% blockage in his right coronary artery. How much scary do you want it to get? Would it take one more call, one more week, or just gearing up to go train? After a stent was placed and several weeks of rehabilitation he successfully passed his stress test and is back on duty. The best person to take care of you, is you.

Second, if you don't have fitness equipment in your station that's fine, you don't need it for cardio anyways. Grab a radio and take laps around the station. One of the new trends that have caught on like wild fire in the Metro Atlanta area is the Cross Fit exercises. You can visit CrossFit.com to find information and they post new exercises every day. During my time in the Gwinnett County Fire Department, they had fully implemented this program in recruit school and most stations are using some form of it. They look at the exercises that are posted and then put a firefighter's modification to it by adding fire service equipment to the exercise. Another option that needs to be explored by all is the annual completion of your department's physical agility test. We all have a responsibility to ensure that everyone can still do the job, not leaving it to chance. Another reference is the Training Officer's Desk Reference by Jones and Bartlett where I dedicated a chapter to Northwest Fire District (Arizona) and Captain Ian Cassidy's recruit school fitness program covers the gamete.

Initiative # 7: Create a national research agenda and data collection system that relates to the initiatives.

Start researching the needs within our stations and departments. Focus on what our crews and firefighters need to be able to safely perform the job. Once we find out what our specific needs are, take them and review the Everyone Goes Home Research Database. The database is a living document that has a vast amount of knowledge about covering all of the initiatives. If you have trouble deciding how or what initiative to implement, this database should be able to help you. Also, it is there for the firefighters, if you find something that works for you then add it to the database. The second part to initiative is start documenting a structure fire as a structure fire. If the house burns down it's not a smoke scare anymore. We cannot justify getting the equipment and manpower that we need if we shoot ourselves in the foot. This will also help us know if we are living the initiatives and making a difference in LODD's.

Initiative #8: Utilize available technology wherever it can produce higher levels of health and safety.

Most of us have cutting edge technology and even if it has a few years on it it's probably still in good condition if it was taken care of. But, we are occasionally failing to use it at all or we are not using it like it was designed. We have gear that keeps a lot of the heat off of us, but we fail to wear it properly, simply not buckling the snap on our helmets and we burn our head. We have thermal imaging cameras in most of our departments but we either don't take it off the truck or don't train on how to interpret images with it. It's a little more than just point and shoot. Apparatus now come with seatbelt extensions for firefighters with their gear on, we have mobile data terminals or laptops, and fancy reflective vest for each of us to wear. Learn how it works and use them, train on them. So, wash your gear, wear your gear, buckle the waist strap and your helmet strap, pull the TIC off, grab a tool, and check all of your equipment out every shift.

Initiative #9: Thoroughly investigate all firefighter fatalities, injuries, and near misses.

If we don't learn from the tragedies that have happened in the past then these firefighters have all died in vain and that is unacceptable. On the other side, it has been proven that one LODD equals 10,000 unsafe acts. We have be better at catching each other's mistakes and learn from them. One particular battalion chief has started requiring every Sunday that crews review at least one LODD report. Firefigternearmiss.com and NIOSH are three excellent sites to visit for information for injuries and fatalities.

Initiative #10: Grant programs should support the implementation of safe practices and/or mandate safe practices as an eligibility requirement.

Initiative #10 is more about the company officers and chief officers but the firefighters can help them achieve it. We need to advocate the need for funding specifically to firefighters and fire departments that want to increase firefighter safety and make a difference. If they can do something with nothing then what could they do with a little money. For firefighters and departments that think that enforcing policies such as wearing your seat belt or stopping at a stop sign or red light is below them, you don't deserve anything. If you do not have SOP's or safe practices in place before the thousands of dollars of new equipment, why would you develop them after the grant?

Initiative #11: National standards for emergency response policies and procedures should be developed and championed.

Our departments need to develop policies and procedures for emergency responses that will mandate safe practices. But, even without a policy, we as firefighters and company officers need to use the common sense we were born with or beat into some of us by our parents and drive the speed limit, stop at all lights, stop at stop signs and WEAR YOUR SEAT BELT!! The whole due regard stuff we hear about, we have to remember our commitment to keeping the citizens safe. There are firefighters serving jail time because of missing one of these items. Will you be next?

Initiative #12: National protocols for response to violent incidents should be developed and championed.

Simply put, we don't carry guns or vest, as least not all of us. Use your common sense and stage so the police can get in and do what they need to do. A couple of examples of what we should be staging at are domestics, drug related, weapons related, and suicide attempt incidents. Stop for a second and gather the whole picture. There are the rare situations like in Gwinnett County recently and in Kentucky a few years back that we cannot change but we can help create policies to keep us safe in most of these events. The epidemic that is occurring in our country right now towards our law enforcement family is disheartening and we should never think we are immune.

On December 1, 2015 a wife of a friend from Portsmouth, Virginia Fire Department wrote an open letter on Facebook to the public that went viral after her husband's fire station was shot at while he was on duty. He is a son, father to two little girls, a husband and fellow brother among so many other things. And, so is his crew. Shortly after the same event occurred in Cleveland, Ohio and earlier in 2016 a rash of vehicle break-ins were occurring in the Charlotte area to private vehicles in the fire station parking lots. I do not have the answers to prevent such occurrences other than to say watch out for each other.

Initiative #13: Firefighters and their families must have access to counseling and psychological support.

Develop an Employee Assistance Program and a Critical Incident Stress Debriefing Program or join an existing region program. But this program shouldn't stop here, our families deal with a lot putting up with most of us; we need to take care of them as well. If nothing else create a support group within your department for the firefighters and one for your families, much like an auxiliary group. Another option would be to create a Fraternal Order Of Leatherheads chapter. I have been a part of two chapters over the years with the main focus being on training and taking care of each other. This way you will have access to resources all across the

United States and a brotherhood to help you. At minimal work on building your crew's camaraderie, this is your support group.

Initiative #14: Public education must receive more resources and be championed as a critical fire and life safety program.

How many public education personnel does your department have? You should be saying everyone in your department. Two or three people are not enough to touch everyone, but with the help of the field personnel we can do some things. Don't wait for the opportunity to come to you though, every time that you're out in the public make it a point to bring some stickers or a helmet and invite the public to your fire house so that you can talk about fire safety. State Farm Insurance will give you materials for free if you will ask for them. The Georgia Firefighters Burn Foundation will give back 10% of our departments annual Boot Drive in the form of prevention materials and smoke detectors. Find out what your Burn Foundation does. It shouldn't be just a week in October. Many departments have devoted the entire month of October, furthermore, in the private sector it is discussed year-round. In the private sector, we have the unique perspective of the fact that if we burn down the facility today many people will not have a job tomorrow. The level of ownership tends to increase with this particular scenario. While I was with Gwinnet County we also had 116 confirmed saves in 2008 due specifically to one fire drill. One of our day care centers had a fairly extensive electrical fire and had to evacuate 116 children and staff. They had practiced the evacuation drill all week getting ready for the firefighters to come the very next day to watch. They cleared the center in 90 seconds with no injuries. How huge is that?

Initiative #15: Advocacy must be strengthened for the enforcement of codes and the installation of home fire sprinklers.

We won a big battle a few years back for the fire service or at least until the Homebuilders Association tried suing the International Code Council because they want to save a dollar. We have to do what former City of Morrow, GA. Fire Chief David Wall did. We have to show the benefits to the people that matter not just talk about them. Chief Wall set up a demonstration, one room with sprinklers and one room without. Once the council members and the public saw how effective the sprinklers were, there were no more questions. Before we can make any progress we have to quit complaining about sprinklers taking away our jobs. You only have to worry about that if you're not doing your job. Next, we have to inform the public about sprinklers. Sprinklers are not extremely expensive, and they will cause less water damage due to their design than if the fire progresses and we stretch a hoseline in. The bottom line is that if we can prevent backdrafts, flashovers and structural collapse our chances of survival and the survival of those we swore to protect is greatly increased. It is people like Chief Shane Ray and Vickie Pritchett who have pushed to envelope and shared their conviction. Part of the NIST/ISFSI studies in Spartanburg were directed specifically at testing fire sprinklers in residential structures and documenting the benefits.

Initiative # 16: Safety must be a primary consideration in the design of apparatus and equipment.

This one can be easy or it can be hard to achieve. If you are purchasing a new apparatus make sure it meets the current NFPA standard. Set up a committee to write the specifications but order four things, seat belt extensions, chevron striping everywhere it can be applied, orange cones, and traffic vest for every seat. Remember that if you don't spec it to the standard, the manufacturer does not have to make it to the standard. Now if you already have an apparatus there are a couple of things that you can do. You can try and bring it up to the current code if money allows. Or you redesign it. Look for heavy equipment in the higher cabinets and bring them lower, think about saving your back due to apparatus design. If your department still has an open cab, don't let anyone ride back there and no riding on the tailboard either. If your department can't afford cones or vest, take your extra house dues and go buy some for the station. Sometimes we may have to adapt and overcome but nothing is impossible.

Appendix 3

Fire Department Leadership: Lessons Learned from the Bible

Many will get this, however, some others may shy away from reading. I admit this is a very different approach for me in my writings. However, I look for purpose and inspiration in everything that I do and this is what I was compelled to write. All of the "stuff" we see throughout our career – sooner or later, we all need that assurance of the higher being and I believe we all want to know that the struggles mattered. As I have continued to read the word of the Bible and attempting to apply to today's society I have complied several lessons learned that I can work towards in bettering myself as a leader and instructor. It is interesting that one of the oldest recorded books in history has some of the greatest leadership and teaching points. Here are a few, I hope you enjoy:

Matthew 25:40   "Assuredly, I say to you in as much as you did it to one the least of these My brethren, you did it to Me."

The point here as a leader is to train your firefighters to be compassionate and to never judge the people who you are there to protect. We typically see people in their worst time, as leaders you have the ability to mold firefighters, and you just never know who you may be taking care of.

Mark 10:27   "With men it is impossible but not with God: for with God all things are possible."

For me, this means to dig deep in my faith. You may be hurt, tired, or sore – but you never give up. You use all of your training and experiences to carry out the next task. As a leader, stress the importance of teamwork. Knowing the strengths and weaknesses of your crew is vital to your success on the incident. One  of my favorite fire truck sayings was witnessed in South Carolina during a training event, it simply stated "Faith in God, Trust in Training."

Luke 14:11   "For whoever exalts himself will be humbled, and he who humbles himself will be exalted."

As a leader, stress that everything is earned and we should never expect anything to be given to us. Those who do not understand this will find out the difficult way, however, those who do understand this will be considered knowledgeable and worth listening too. These are the people we all enjoy working for.

John 15:13   "Greater love has no one than this, than to lay down one's life for his friends."

We have the responsibility to be role models in every aspect; from fitness to knowledge to training. The veterans must show the way and provide a clear path for the younger generation. Because, we should never forget what it really means to wear the badge and to protect your brothers and sisters. And, when we think about RIC, it is not just a meaningless job when you put it in perspective.

Romans 5:3-4   "And not only that, but we also glory in tribulations, knowing that tribulation produces perseverance; and perseverance, character; and character, hope.

Do not give up when times get tough; stand firm, be a better person and have faith in a better tomorrow. Challenge yourself to be stronger and smarter everyday through developing experiences by training and asking for the difficult assignments. The more we experience today, the better prepared we are for tomorrow.

I Corinthians 6:8   "Therefore, if food makes my brother stumble, I will never again eat meat, lest I make my brother fail."

This phrase has nothing to do with food but has everything to do with formal and informal leaders. It simply means, do not let your actions or inactions lead your brother or sister to failure. If you are looked up to, in any capacity, use it for good and develop your crew - you will never know when you will depend on your brothers and sisters.

I Corinthians 15:33   "Evil company corrupts good habits."

This is an interesting quote but very true. It is hard enough to fight against what is easy and settling for the status quo within ourselves. Train your crew to stand tall and remember their principles. If we live by faith and principles, we will not be tempted by the bad company – we will be disciplined.

References

Ashbroft, D. Micheal., (2002). *Management Techniques for the Best Damn Ship in the Navy*. New York, New York. Warner Business Books

Brown, Karen A., and Hyer, Nancy L., (2010). *Managing Projects*. McGraw-Hill Education.

Brunacini, Alan. (2015, October). Fire Engineering. *Expectations and Boundaries, 168*, 10.

Brunacini, Alan. (2015, June). Fire Engineering. *More Power Goofs, 168*, 6.

Brunacini, Alan. (2014, April). Fire Engineering. *No Brainer Management, Part 4: Tell Me What You Want, 167*, 4.

Brunacini, Alan. (2014, July). Fire Engineering. *No Brainer Management, Part 7: Organizational Alignment, 167*, 7.

Bullard, David. (2015, January). Georgia Firefighter. *Lassiez vs. Lazy, 42*, 1.

Crocker III, W. H., and Goldman, Ed. (2000). *Robert E. Lee on Leadership: Executive Lessons in Character, Courage, and Vision*. New York, New York. Three Rivers Press

Manning, G., and K. Curtis., *The Art of Leadership* (2nd ed.) New York: McGraw-Hill/Irwin, 2007.

DeSimone, Randy L. and Werner, Jon M.., (2012). *Human Resource Development*. Mason, OH. South-Western

Dittmann, Melissa. (June 2005). Generational Difference at Work. *Monitor on Psychology*. Vol 36, No 6. Retrieved from http://www.apa.org/monitor/jun05/generational.aspx

Enright, E. J and Glosser, Kurt. (2014, July). Fire Engineering. *The Maltese Cross: Virtues for Today's Fire Service. 167*, 4.

Everyone Goes Home. Retrieved June 23, 2015. Retrieved from http://www.everyonegoeshome.com/.

Firehistory.org. Retrieved on June 19, 2015. Retrieved from http://www.fireserviceinfo.com/history.html.

Halton, Bobby. (2015, November). Fire Engineering. *The Character of Stirring Symbols, 168,* 11.

Halton, Bobby. (2014, July). Fire Engineering. *The Rhythm, 167,* 7

Hartin, Ed. Estimating Required Fire Flow: The Iowa Formula. Retrieved on August 1, 2015. Retrieved from http://cfbt-us.com/wordpress/?p=75

Hartin, Ed. Estimating Required Fire Flow: The National Fire Academy Formula. Retrieved on August 1, 2015. Retrieved from http://cfbt-us.com/wordpress/?p=74

Hartley, Joey. (2014, Winter). Georgia Firefighter. *Where Do I Go Next?, 41,* 1

Georgia Smoke Divers. Retrieved on July 25, 2015. Retrieved from http://www.georgiasmokediver.com/.

Kastros, Anthony (2014, July). Fire Engineering. *The American Fire Service Leadership Pandemic, 167,* 4.

Klein, Gary., (1998). *Sources of Power.* Cambridge, Massachusetts. MIT Press

Klein, Gary., (2003). *Power of Intuition.* New York, NY. Double Day

Klein, Gary and Zsambok, Caroline E., (1996). *Naturalistic Decision Making.* New York, NY. Routledge

Lasky, Rick. (2006). *Pride and Ownership*. Tulsa, Oklahoma. Pennwell Corporation

Marquet, David. L. (2012). *Turn the Ship Around*. New York, New York. Penguin Group

Marano, Hara. E. (2008). *A Nation of Wimps*. New York, New York. Broadway Books.

Metro Atlanta Firefighter Conference. Retrieved on April 15, 2015. Retrieved from http://www.everyonegoeshome.com/.

Mills, Steven (2014, July). Fire Engineering. *Sizing Up the Fireground Leader: How Do You Measure Up?, 167, 7*.

Powell, L. C., *My American Journey*. New York: Random House, 1995.

Salka, John. (2004). *First In, Last Out*. New York, New York. Penguin Group

Shriberg, David and Shriberg, Arthur (2011). *Practicing Leadership: Principles and Applications*. Hoboken, New Jersey. John Wiley and Sons Inc.

Swafford, Lanier. (2014, Winter). Georgia Firefighter. *Stand Up and Be Counted, 41*, 1.

Thompson, J. Scott., (2014, April). Fire Engineering. *Training Basics, 167*, 4.

Training Resources and Data Exchange. Retrieved on June 20, 2015. Retrieved from http://www.usfa.fema.gov/training/nfa/programs/trade.html.

University of Texas Fire Prevention. Retrieved on July 25, 2015. Retrieved from http://www.utexas.edu/safety/fire/safety/historic_fires.html.

U.S. Army Field Manual (FM) 6-22, *Army Leadership* (Washington, DC: U.S.
Government Printing Office [GPO], October 2006.), 1-2.

U.S. Air Force Doctrine Document 1-1, *Leadership and Force Development* (Washington, DC: US. Government Printing Office [GPO], November 2011.

Viscuso, Frank. (2014, July). Fire Engineering. *Mentoring for Success, 167*, 7

Ward, Brian J., (2014). *Training Officer's Desk Reference.* Burlington, MA. Jones and Bartlett Learning

Ward, Brian J., (2012). *Always be prepared for the Unexpected.* Fire Engineering

Ward, Brian J. (2008). *Leadership from the Little Guy.* Retrieved on July 25, 2015. Retrieved from http://www.fireengineering.com/articles/2008/09/leadership-from-the-little-guy.html.

Ward, Brian J.; Rhodes, David (2011). *Mentoring: Perspectives of a Rookie and the Veteran Firefighter.* Retrieved from www.FireEngineering.com

Ward, Brian J. (2009). *Saving Lives One Initiative at a Time. Retrieved on April 15, 2015.* Retrieved from http://www.fireengineering.com/articles/2009/06/saving-firefighter-lives-one-initiative-at-a-time-a-gloves-off-approach.html

Ward, Brian J. (2011). *LODD: What to do the prevent a LODD?.* Fire Engineering

Ward, Brian J. (2008). *Talkin' about my Generation.* Retrieved on May 13, 2015. Retrieved from http://www.firerescue1.com/cod-company-officer-development/articles/435815-Talkin-bout-my-generation/.

Ward, Brian J. (2013). *Hiring Experienced Firefighters During Tough Times.* Fire Engineering

About the Author

Brian J. Ward

After serving as a facility chief of emergency operations, Brian was promoted to Divisional Compliance System Owner for Fire Protection and Emergency Operations, Georgia Pacific – Plywood Division. Brian has served as the International Society of Fire Service Instructors (ISFSI) Director At Large for the past four years and as a member of the ISFSI Executive Board the last two years. Brian has been instrumental in the delivery of the ISFSI 1403 Live Fire Credentialing Program as a Lead Instructor and Vice-Chair since its inception, a member of the Principles of Modern Fire Attack Instructor Cadre, Managing Editor for the Jones and Bartlett Training Officer's Desk Reference and Program Manager for the ISFSI Training Officer's Credentialing Program in partnership with Columbia Southern University. Brian received his Bachelor's Degree in Fire Safety and Technology Engineering from the University of Cincinnati, is Certified Georgia Smoke Diver #741 and is currently pursuing his Master's in Organizational Leadership from Columbia Southern University.

Brian has received several honors including: Fire Department Management from National Association of Counties, Distinguished Service Award, Firefighter of the Year, Top 20 CTBS Instructor and National Seal of Excellence for Leadership and Safety from the National Fallen Fighters Foundation and several ISFSI Organizational Awards and the ISFSI Presidential Award in 2016. Brian has served on the Honeywell First Responder Advisory Council, Chairman of the Metro Atlanta Training Officers Association and the AFG Criteria Development Committee.

Currently, Brian is working with Fire Engineering on the Training Officer's Toolbox publishing bi-monthly one page lesson plans on various topics. Brian has authored over 35 nationally publicized articles and research papers, in addition to speaking engagements across the country on training and emergency response topics. Brian has experience as a classroom, workshop and hands-on-training instructor at FDIC. Lastly, thanks to my wonderful wife for allowing me to do all of this!

Take Care, Train Hard and Be Safe!

Brian

Made in the USA
Lexington, KY
21 January 2017